A GUIDE TO

ENDURING
LOVE

A GUIDE TO

ENDURING LOVE

JANE EASTON
WITH TONY BUZAN

Hodder & Stoughton

ISBN 0 340 80303 7

First published 2001
Impression number   10 9 8   7 6   5 4 3 2
Year   2006 2005 2004 2003 2002

The 'Teach Yourself' name and logo are registered trade marks of
Hodder & Stoughton Ltd.

Cover photograph: Corel Photo Library
Illustrations: David Ashby
Mind Maps: Kate Boyd

Typeset by Transet Limited, Coventry, England.
Printed in Great Britain for Hodder & Stoughton Educational, a division of
Hodder Headline Plc, 338 Euston Road, London NW1 3BH by Cox and Wyman Ltd,
Reading, Berks.

CONTENTS

REVISION FOR A-LEVEL LITERATURE SUCCESS

You are now in the most important educational stage of your life, and are soon to take English Literature exams that may have a major impact on your future career and goals. As one A-level student put it: 'It's crunch time!'

At this crucial stage of your life the one thing you need even more than subject knowledge is the knowledge of *how* to remember, *how* to read faster, *how* to comprehend, *how* to study, *how* to take notes and *how* to organize your thoughts. You need to know how to *think*; you need a basic introduction on how to use that super bio-computer inside your head – your brain.

The next eight pages contain a goldmine of information on how you can achieve success both at school and in your A-level English Literature exams, as well as in your professional or university career. These eight pages will give you skills that will enable you to be successful in *all* your academic pursuits. You will learn:

◆ How to recall more *while* you are learning.
◆ How to recall more *after* you have finished a class or a study period.
◆ How to use special techniques to improve your memory.
◆ How to use a revolutionary note-taking technique called Mind Maps that will double your memory and help you to write essays and answer exam questions.
◆ How to read everything faster while at the same time improving your comprehension and concentration.
◆ How to zap your revision!

How to understand, improve and master your memory of Literature Guides

Your memory really is like a muscle. Don't exercise it and it will grow weaker; *do* exercise it properly and it will grow incredibly more powerful. There are really only four main things you need to understand about your memory in order to increase its power dramatically:

Recall during learning
– YOU MUST TAKE BREAKS!

When you are studying, your memory can concentrate, understand and recall well for between 20 and 45 minutes at a time. Then it *needs* a break. If you carry on for longer than this without one, your memory starts to break down. If you study for hours non-stop, you will remember only a fraction of what you have been trying to learn, and you will have wasted valuable revision time.

So, ideally, *study for less than an hour*, then take a five- to ten-minute break. During this break listen to music, go for a walk, do some exercise, or just daydream. (Daydreaming is a necessary brain-power booster – geniuses do it regularly.) During the break your brain will be sorting out what it has been learning and you will go back to your study with the new information safely stored and organized in your memory banks. Make *sure* you take breaks at regular intervals as you work through the *Literature Guides*.

Recall after learning
– SURFING THE WAVES OF YOUR MEMORY

What do you think begins to happen to your memory straight *after* you have finished learning something? Does it immediately start forgetting? No! Surprisingly, your brain actually *increases* its power and carries on remembering. For a short time after your study session, your brain integrates the information, making a more complete picture of everything it has just learnt. Only then does the rapid decline in memory begin, as much as 80 per cent of what you have learnt can be forgotten in a day.

However, if you catch the top of the wave of your memory, and briefly review what you have been revising at the correct time, the memory is stamped in far more strongly, and stays at the crest of the wave for a much longer time. To maximize your brain's power to remember, take a few minutes and use a Mind Map to review what you have learnt at the end of a day. Then review it at the end of a week, again at the end of a month, and finally a week before the exams. That way you'll surf-ride your memory wave all the way to your exam, success and beyond!

The memory principle of association

The muscle of your memory becomes stronger when it can **associate** – when it can link things together.

Think about your best friend, and all the things your mind *automatically* links with that person. Think about your favourite hobby, and all the associations your mind has when you think about (remember!) that hobby.

When you are studying, use this memory principle to make associations between the elements in your subjects, and thus to improve both your memory and your chances of success.

The memory principle of imagination

The muscle of your memory will improve significantly if you can produce big images in your mind. Rather than just memorizing the name of a character, imagine that character of the novel or play as if you were a video producer filming that person's life. The same goes for images in poetry.

In *all* your subjects use the **imagination** memory principle.

Throughout this *Literature Guide* you will find special association and imagination techniques (called mnemonics after the Greek goddess Mnemosyne) that will make it much easier for you to remember the topic being discussed. Look out for them!

Your new success formula: Mind Maps®

You have noticed that when people go on holidays, or travel, they take maps. Why? To give them a general picture of where they are going, to help them locate places of special interest and importance, to help them find things more easily, and to help them remember distances and locations, etc.

It is exactly the same with your mind and with study. If you have a 'map of the territory' of what you have to learn, then everything is easier. In learning and study, the Mind Map is that special tool.

As well as helping you with all areas of study, the Mind Map actually *mirrors the way your brain works.* Your Mind Maps can be used for taking notes from your study books, for taking notes in class, for preparing your homework, for presenting your homework, for reviewing your tests, for checking your and your friends' knowledge in any subject, and for *helping you understand anything you learn.* Mind Maps are especially useful in English literature, as they allow you to map out the whole territory of a novel, play or poem, giving you an 'at-a-glance' snapshot of all the key information you need to know.

The Mind Maps in the *Literature Guide* use, throughout, **imagination** and **association.** As such, they automatically strengthen your memory muscle every time you use them. Throughout this guide you will find Mind Maps that summarize the most important areas of the English Literature guide you are studying. Study these Mind Maps, add some colour, personalize them, and then have a go at making your own Mind Maps of the work you are studying – you will remember them far better! Put them on your walls and in your files for a quick and easy review. Mind Maps are fast, efficient, effective and, importantly, *fun* to do!

HOW TO DRAW A MIND MAP

1 Start in the middle of the page with the page turned sideways. This gives your brain more radiant freedom for its thoughts.

2 Always start by drawing a picture or symbol of the novel or its title. Why? Because *a picture is worth a thousand words to your brain*. Try to use at least three colours, as colour helps your memory even more.

3 Let your thoughts flow, and write or draw your ideas on coloured branching lines connected to your central image. The key symbols and words are the headings for your topic.

4 Next, add facts and ideas by drawing more, smaller, branches on to the appropriate main branches, just like a tree.

5 Always print your word clearly on its line. Use only one word per line.

6 To link ideas and thoughts on different branches, use arrows, colours, underlining and boxes.

HOW TO READ A MIND MAP

1 Begin in the centre, the focus of your novel, play or poem.

2 The words/images attached to the centre are like chapter headings; read them next.

3 Always read out from the centre, in every direction (even on the left-hand side, where you will read from right to left, instead of the usual left to right).

USING MIND MAPS

Mind Maps are a versatile tool – use them for taking notes in class or from books, for solving problems, for brainstorming with friends, and for reviewing and revising for exams – their uses are infinite! You will find them invaluable for planning essays for coursework and exams. Number your main branches in the order in which you want to use them and off you go – the main headings for your essay are done and all your ideas are logically organized!

Super speed reading and study

What do you think happens to your comprehension as your reading speed rises? 'It goes down!' Wrong! It seems incredible, but it has been proved – the faster you read, the more you comprehend and remember!

So here are some tips to help you to practise reading faster – you'll cover the ground much more quickly, remember more, *and* have more time for revision and leisure activities!

SUPER SPEED READING

1 First read the whole text (whether it's a lengthy book or an exam paper) very quickly, to give your brain an overall idea of what's ahead and get it working. (It's like sending out a scout to look at the territory you have to cover – it's much easier when you know what to expect!) Then read the text again for more detailed information.
2 Have the text a reasonable distance away from your eyes. In this way your eye/brain system will be able to see more at a glance, and will naturally begin to read faster.
3 Take in groups of words at a time. Rather than reading 'slowly and carefully' read faster, more enthusiastically. Your comprehension will rocket!
4 Take in phrases rather than single words while you read.
5 Use a guide. Your eyes are designed to follow movement, so a thin pencil underneath the lines you are reading, moved smoothly along, will 'pull' your eyes to faster speeds.

HOW TO MAKE STUDY EASY FOR YOUR BRAIN

When you are going somewhere, is it easier to know beforehand where you are going, or not? Obviously it is easier if you *do* know. It is the same for your brain and a book. When you get a new book, there are seven things you can do to help your brain get to 'know the territory' faster:

1 Scan through the whole book in less than 20 minutes, as you would do if you were in a shop thinking whether or not to buy it. This gives your brain *control*.

2 Think about what you already know about the subject. You'll often find out it's a lot more than you thought. A good way of doing this is to do a quick Mind Map on *everything you know* after you have skimmed through it.

3 Ask who, what, why, where, when and how questions about what is in the book. Questions help your brain 'fish' the knowledge out.

4 Ask your friends what they know about the subject. This helps them review the knowledge in their own brains, and helps your brain get new knowledge about what you are studying.

5 Have another quick speed read through the book, this time looking for any diagrams, pictures and illustrations, and also at the beginnings and ends of chapters. Most information is contained in the beginnings and ends.

6 If you come across any difficult parts in your book, mark them and *move on.* Your brain *will* be able to solve the problems when you come back to them a bit later. Much like saving the difficult bits of a jigsaw puzzle for later. When you have finished the book, quickly review it one more time and then discuss it with friends. This will lodge it permanently in your memory banks.

7 Build up a Mind Map as you study the book. This helps your brain to organize and hold (remember!) information as you study.

Helpful hints for exam revision

◆ To avoid **exam panic** cram at the *start* of your course, not the end. It takes the same amount of time, so you may as well use it where it is best placed!

◆ Use Mind Maps throughout your course, and build a Master Mind Map for each subject – a giant Mind Map that summarizes everything you know about the subject.

◆ Use memory techniques such as mnemonics (verses or systems for remembering things like dates and events or lists).

◆ Get together with one or two friends to revise, compare Mind Maps, and discuss topics.

AND FINALLY ...

◆ *Have fun while you learn* – studies show that those people who enjoy what they are doing understand and remember it more, and generally do better.

◆ *Use your teachers* as resource centres. Ask them for help with specific topics and with more general advice on how you can improve your all-round performance.

◆ *Personalize your* **Literature Revision Guide** by underlining and highlighting, by adding notes and pictures. Allow your brain to have a conversation with it!

Your amazing brain and its amazing cells

Your brain is like a super, *super, SUPER* computer. The world's best computers have only a few thousand or hundred thousand computer chips. Your brain has 'computer chips' too, and they are called brain cells. Unlike the computer, you do not have only a few thousand computer chips – the number of brain cells in your head is a *million MILLION*!! This means you are a genius just waiting to discover yourself! All you have to do is learn how to get those brain cells working together, and you'll not only become more smart, you'll have more free time to pursue your other fun activities.

The more you understand your amazing brain the more it will repay and amaze you!

Apply its power to this *Literature Guide*!

(Tony Buzan)

HOW TO USE THIS GUIDE

This guide assumes that you have already read *Enduring Love*, although you could read 'The story of *Enduring Love*' first. It is best to use the guide alongside the novel. You will get the most out of the 'Characterization' and 'Themes' sections if you refer to the novel.

The sections

The 'Commentary' section can be used in several ways. One way is to read a chapter of the novel, and then read the relevant commentary. Keep on until you come to a test section, test yourself – then have a break! Alternatively, read the commentary for a chapter, then read that chapter in the novel, then return to the commentary. See what works best for you.

'Critical approaches' gives some ideas about literary criticism and looks at a few reviews of the novel. Your own response is important, but be aware of these approaches too.

'How to get an "A" in English Literature' gives valuable advice on how to approach a text, and what skills to develop in order to achieve your personal best.

'The exam essay' is a useful 'night before' reminder of how to tackle exam questions, though it will help you more if you also look at it much earlier in the year. 'Model answer' gives an example A-grade essay and the Mind Map and plan used to write it.

The questions

Whenever you come across a question in the guide with a star ❖ in front of it, think about it for a moment. You could make a Mini Mind Map or a few notes to focus your mind. There is not usually a 'right' answer to these: it is important for you to develop your own opinions if you want to get an 'A'. The 'Test' sections are designed to take you 15–20 minutes each – time well spent. Take a short break after each one.

Page references

Page references in this guide are to the Vintage paperback edition.

 EY TO ICONS

Themes

A **theme** is an idea explored by an author. Whenever a theme is dealt with in the guide, the appropriate icon is used. This means you can find where a theme is mentioned by flicking through the book. Go on – try it now!

Science		Religion and spirituality	
Love		Fate	
Keats the poet		Disease and illness	
Morality		Children	

 LANGUAGE, STYLE AND STRUCTURE

This heading and icon are used in the 'Commentary' wherever there is a special section on the author's choice of words and imagery, and the overall plot structure.

The author

Ian McEwan has written novels and short stories since the 1970s and is regarded as one of the UK's finest contemporary writers. Two of his early works, *The Cement Garden* and *The Comfort of Strangers*, have been made into films. A recent novel, *Amsterdam*, won the 1998 Booker Prize, the UK's most prestigious fiction award. *Enduring Love* was published in 1997.

McEwan's earlier writing explores the darker side of human behaviour and has earned him the nickname 'Ian Macabre'. *The Cement Garden* is a good example of this, being about four children who try to conceal the death of their mother by burying her in the garden. His later work is less brooding, but as *Enduring Love* demonstrates, he continues to take a long, hard look at so-called 'normal' life.

Influences on Enduring Love

THE ENLIGHTENMENT

It is helpful to have some understanding of the Enlightenment in order to follow the novel's debate about rational thought versus spirituality. Although McEwan does not refer to it directly, the ideas that came out of the Enlightenment helped to shape modern life as we know it. Some of its ideas form Joe's viewpoint about the world because he is from a scientific background.

The Enlightenment is the name given to one of the most important European intellectual movements. Its followers believed in scientific and rational enquiry, and freedom from superstition. The movement reached its peak during the mid-eighteenth century, but its influence continued long afterwards. The Enlightenment was part of a reaction against the religious persecution and intolerance that had held back important discoveries in science. Although some of us may feel less optimistic now about the achievements of scientific progress, it was once hoped that science could 'cure' backward ideas and behaviour. Great thinkers believed that humans could become rational, thinking beings and improve the world with scientific and philosophical discoveries – instead of being controlled by religious superstition and fear.

Writers and scientists who inspired or shaped the Enlightenment include Descartes, Locke, Newton, Voltaire and Rousseau.

THE ROMANTICS

This is another period of intellectual thought that influences some of the important themes in the novel. When you see this word or one of its roots beginning with a capital letter, it has a different meaning to the everyday one of 'love'. The Romantic Movement was a literary movement that took place in Europe between the late eighteenth and early nineteenth centuries. Its ideas were very influential, not just in intellectual circles.

Romanticism was partly inspired by the wave of political revolutions that took place in America and France around this period. There were many ideas about how society could become more fair and equal. Most importantly, Romanticism had an emotional basis, believing in the value of individual experience. Its other important feature was that it was concerned with a sense of the infinite and the transcendental. In other words, it believed that there was more to life than those things that could be proved by science – there were cosmic and natural forces that shaped our lives, though not necessarily religious in a conventional Christian way. The Romantics were particularly interested in the idea of 'Imagination' and the way it could transform our lives.

The Romantic Movement was partly a reaction to the Enlightenment, the previous set of ideas that had swept Europe in the earlier part of the eighteenth century. The Romantics were not necessarily anti-science, however; they just thought that other approaches to the world were as important, if not more so. Key Romantic writers other than Keats include the poets Wordsworth, Coleridge and Byron, and the novelist Mary Shelley (author of *Frankenstein*). Romantic literature is full of lonely characters pursuing elusive goals – a bit like Jed Parry pursuing the love of Joe Rose, perhaps? And of course, Clarissa is an expert in the works of Keats.

KEATS

Keats was born in 1795 and died from tuberculosis in 1821, aged only 26. His work was not well received during his short life, but he is now accepted as one of Britain's most important poets. His letters are also regarded as important works of literature.

Keats is particularly famous for his ideas on 'Negative Capability'. Roughly speaking, this can be defined as a state of mind in which someone is 'capable of being in uncertainties, mysteries, doubts, without any irritable reaching after fact and reason'. This is quite a different way of looking at the world compared to Joe's questioning attitude and is perhaps closer to Clarissa's approach to life. Keats' view suggests that there may be things which we can never fully unravel, but which we can just accept – and perhaps even enjoy – as mysterious contradictions. ❂ What do you think? Do Keats and Clarissa have the right idea, or is Joe correct to question everything?

Most Europeans were Christian in Keats' time, although there were many different branches of the religion. Keats was sceptical of organized religion, but spiritual nonetheless. He stated that he was 'certain of nothing but the holiness of the Heart's affections and the truth of the Imagination.' In other words, he was not convinced about anything but love and the power of creative imagination. This is a form of what we would now call 'humanism' – in other words, humans are enough in themselves and are not just depraved creatures that can only be saved by God. (Keats' ideas would have been regarded as rather blasphemous at the time although they are common today.)

The language of Keats' poetry has been described as 'sensuously descriptive' – the very sounds of his words were meant to stimulate the senses. His poems present states of 'luxurious ease and torpor'; almost trancelike states of relaxation. He also believed in the idea of 'art for art's sake' – in other words, that art should not have to be useful or explain itself; it can just exist as a thing of beauty.

Another famous idea of his, from the poem 'Ode to a Grecian Urn' is that 'beauty is truth, truth beauty.' Not everyone agrees with Keats on this; it can seem very naïve. Not all truth is beautiful and not everything that is beautiful is necessarily the truth.

Get into context!

? Make a Mini Mind Map of the three areas covered in the 'Context' section. This will help your understanding and recall of these new ideas.

? Romantics v. Enlightenment-ers! List the good and bad points of the two different movements. If you are studying with a friend, have a debate.

Catastrophe

The opening chapter describes a shocking accident. Joe and his long-term partner Clarissa Mellon are settling down to their picnic when they hear shouting, then see an air balloon coming down across the field. They rush to help, and meet up with four men: John Logan, Toby Greene, Joseph Lacey and Jed Parry. The five men ignore advice from the pilot, James Gadd, whose grandson Harry is trapped in the balloon. Instead, they all try to hang on to the balloon ropes. Gusts of wind force all but John Logan to let go. He hangs on and is swept high into the air, then falls from the rope and is killed. As with most of the novel, the account of the accident is given in the first person by a central character, Joe Rose.

Aftershock

There is a brief encounter between Jed Parry and Joe, when Parry wants them to pray, but Joe thinks little of it at that point. Upon arriving home, Clarissa and Joe go over the accident, trying to come to terms with it. Joe feels guilty because he wonders if Logan could have been saved if they had all hung on. Later, he is woken by an unexpected phone call from Jed Parry, whose voice he recognizes. Parry says that he understands Joe's feelings and that he loves Joe. However, Joe lies to Clarissa about the call, saying that it was a wrong number.

Stalking

The first phone call from Parry is followed by many more. Later, Joe is doing research work in a library when he gets the feeling that he is being watched by Parry. Joe does not tell Clarissa about these incidents for a few days. When he does so, she does not believe that it is serious. Next, he agrees to meet with Parry, who has been phoning him near Joe's house. Parry believes that the glance they exchanged immediately after the balloon accident had special meaning – he interprets it as a religious sign. Joe convinces himself that Parry is just a lonely eccentric, but changes his mind after receiving further phone calls and harassment. He makes a complaint to the police but is not taken seriously.

Relationship under strain

When Clarissa returns home in Chapter 9, Joe changes from narrator and writes the chapter through her eyes. She has not glimpsed Parry since the accident and Joe has erased the thirty answerphone messages from him. Clarissa has had a bad day at work, including the loss of her appointment diary. She finds Joe's behaviour manic and insensitive. It is clear that she believes the shock of the accident is making him irrational. When he leaves the flat in a rage after their argument, he is followed by Parry, who issues curses and threats, and accuses Joe of leading him on.

Mind of a stalker

Chapter 11 is written in the form of an intense, poetic letter from Jed Parry, expressing his love for Joe and explaining his feelings. He believes that Joe has left him special 'messages' such as the *energy* that he claims Joe left behind on a bush. Parry takes it for granted that Joe will leave Clarissa for him, another sign of his obsession. We learn that he recently inherited a large sum of money and an expensive house.

Things fall apart

The gap between the couple widens and Joe becomes irrationally fearful that Clarissa is using the situation to hide an affair. He even searches through her desk. During this difficult time Joe also experiences regrets about leaving scientific research for journalism: his whole world is being turned upside down, making him question the purpose of his life.

Joe also visits Jean Logan because he feels guilty about her husband's death. She is bitter because she believes that John was having an affair. Her children play noisily behind the curtains while she talks. The curtain game triggers a memory in Joe, leading him to suspect that Parry is suffering from a form of mental illness called de Clérambault's syndrome.

Back in London, Parry is waiting for him with copies of every article Joe has ever written. He is angry about the rational ideas expressed in Joe's writings and continues by making a vague threat to Joe: *'I can get people to do things for me. Anything I want.'* When Joe returns to the flat, Clarissa confronts him about spying on her.

Faith versus science

Parry writes another letter to Joe after reading the articles. He accuses Joe of arrogance and sadness, claiming that his scientific rationality cuts him off from religious love. There are further vague threats and he ends in an ominous way: *'Never try to pretend to yourself that I do not exist.'*

The rot sets in

Clarissa and Joe drift further apart, paralysed by doubt and shame. Parry continues to stalk Joe and send him letters. Realizing the extent of Parry's obsession, Joe becomes more afraid and wonders how he might defend himself. Despite his own problems he tries to help Jean Logan uncover the truth about her husband.

Clarissa breaks the silence by telling Joe that their relationship is over. After she suggests that Joe is ill and hints that he may have written the letters himself, he realizes that he will have to deal with the stalker on his own. Joe edits Parry's letters to emphasize the veiled threats contained in them and takes them to the police. Inspector Linley fails to be convinced by Joe's fears, and fobs him off. On his way to make preparations for Clarissa's birthday, Joe thinks fondly of the previous year and how close they once were. Joe realizes that the job of mending their relationship will have to be his alone. He feels isolated.

Birthday bloodbath

At the restaurant where they celebrate Clarissa's birthday, Joe gives her an expensive first edition of Keats' poems. As he takes part in the celebrations, he becomes aware of other people around him. These details are very vague, rather like glimpsing something out of the corner of one's eye, but Joe's repeated references to hindsight reinforce the sense of danger. Unaware of the danger about to strike, the three diners make interesting conversation. Clarissa's godfather, Jocelyn Kale, tells the story of the discovery of DNA and they discuss a famous story about Keats and Wordsworth.

Two men then approach a table near to where Clarissa and Joe are seated and shoot a man, Colin Tapp. Joe sees Parry leap from his seat elsewhere in the restaurant, disarm the gunman then disappear. He is convinced that Parry hired the killers to murder him, and that they shot the wrong man.

Aftermath

Despite Joe's evidence, the police do not believe him and repeat that he needs psychiatric help. He believes that he is in serious danger, so decides to buy a gun. In desperation he enlists the help of an old friend, the shady Johnny B. On their return to London after a dangerous but amusing episode with the owners of the gun, Clarissa phones Joe. Parry has broken into the flat and is holding her prisoner. Joe gets into the flat and discovers that Parry has a knife. He seems about to harm himself, but Joe takes no chances and shoots him. Despite all this, he and Clarissa are not reunited immediately. She is shocked by the shooting and believes that Joe may have provoked Parry by overreacting at the beginning of the stalking.

Ten days later, Joe and Clarissa meet up with Jean Logan and her children, Rachael and Leo. A couple arrives: James Reid and Bonny Deedes. They tell Jean that John Logan had given them a lift just before the accident – it was their picnic remains that were found in his car. They convince Jean of her late husband's faithfulness. She now has to cope with her own guilt at mistrusting John. The main part of the novel ends with the children mending their quarrel – a hopeful sign for Clarissa and Joe. Rachel asks Joe to tell them both about how the river 'works'.

Fiction or non-fiction?

Appendix I is written in the style of a psychiatric paper on de Clérambault's syndrome. It explains the symptoms then gives a 'case study', that of Jed Parry's obsession with Joe Rose. From it, we learn that Parry stole Clarissa's diary then used the information to send hired killers to the restaurant. The crime was bungled when the gunmen shot the wrong man. Parry is imprisoned in a psychiatric hospital with no hope of cure. Joe and Clarissa are later reconciled and adopt a child.

Appendix II concludes the novel with a letter from Jed Parry in which he repeats his love for Joe – one of many letters that we know will never be posted by the hospital.

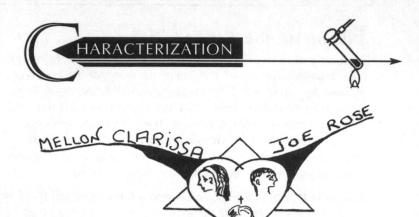

CHARACTERIZATION

The Mini Mind Map above summarizes the main characters in *Enduring Love*. When you have read this section, look at the full Mind Map on p. 17, then make a copy of the Mini Mind Map and try to add to it from memory. A list of minor characters has also been included at the end of this section.

McEwan's characters are established through their words and actions and also by the changing narrative viewpoint. We are given a brief description of Jed Parry in Chapter 2, but references to Joe and Clarissa's appearance are few and far between.

Joe Rose

Joe, the main narrator of the novel, is a scientist turned science journalist. He describes himself as *a large, clumsy, balding fellow*. Other than this, there is little detail about his physical appearance. Instead, we learn a lot about the way he thinks and feels – his inner life. He and Clarissa have been together for seven years. They have no children because Clarissa is unable to get pregnant. Despite their sorrow over this, they have a satisfying and happy life.

Joe is a rational man whose orderly life is turned upside down when Jed Parry develops an obsession with him. For Joe, their meeting at the site of the accident is simply by chance, whereas Jed believes that God brought them together. This difference in outlook forms one of the main themes in the novel, namely the conflict between science and religion. In a letter to Joe, Jed Parry tells him that *without God's love you are living in a desert.* In fact, Ian McEwan himself disagrees with this point of view, stating that it is possible to feel awe and wonder at the world without believing that a conscious force – God – created it. ✪ What do you think – is Joe cut off from the wonders of life because he is not religious?

Whatever you think about Joe, it is probably safe to say that he is sometimes emotionally unaware. Remember that a lot of what he says is written from hindsight and after long discussions with Clarissa about his behaviour. He does not always use his heart and his head at the same time. Look also at the differences between the couple, because they are crucial to the outcome of the novel. Joe is talented and intelligent but dissatisfied with what he does. He would like to go back to pure science, but he has been away from it too long. Clarissa on the other hand, is a Keats scholar who 'on the whole' enjoys her work. Their different occupations may be said to represent the split between science and Romanticism. Science is based on what we can prove with evidence, whereas Romanticism is more concerned with what we feel.

One incident that tells us a lot about Joe is when he lies to Clarissa about Parry's first phone call. He also wipes off the numerous messages on their answerphone. It makes his claims about Parry's persecution more difficult for her to believe – why didn't he tell her at the time? Joe may have been trying to 'protect' Clarissa from worry, but by not sharing this important information he creates a division between them.

As well as his manic behaviour immediately after John Logan's death, we see him acting strangely on other occasions. By the time he does tell her about Jed Parry, his behaviour has worried her so much that she thinks that the accident has disturbed him. She wonders if it is he who is obsessed with Parry, not the other way round.

In Chapter 9, the chapter written by Joe from Clarissa's point of view, he is described as *talking but barely self-aware* and also, that his *precise and careful mind ... takes no account of its own emotional field. He seems unaware that his arguments are no more than ravings.* Joe's lack of self-awareness at times of crisis is one thing that drives a wedge between him and Clarissa.

Clarissa Mellon

Clarissa is an intelligent woman with a successful academic career. Her speciality is Romantic literature, especially Keats. She enjoys her job and is generally inspired by what she does, despite the occasional bad day at work. There is little description of her, but it is clear that Joe finds her beautiful. He describes her *Celt's pale skin and green eyes.* She is romantic in a conventional sense, in that she wrote Joe passionate and beautiful love letters in the first few months of their relationship.

She is a modern middle-class woman, educated and financially independent. She and Joe are very much equals. She loves him deeply and is not embarrassed to show it. *'Joe. I've wanted you all day,'* she declares after a difficult meeting with her brother.

Clarissa is fearful of madness, like many of us. When she was a child, her father died of Alzheimer's disease (a condition that affects a person's mental and physical faculties). *That's why she chose rational Joe.* His rational approach is one of the qualities she loves about him, although she can become irritated by it at times. Indeed, she says *'you're so rational sometimes you're like a child.'* In other words, she thinks that a child's logic can make one miss out on a deeper understanding. (Yet children use their minds to 'dig down' in order to understand the world around them!) Clarissa is not superstitious or anti-intellectual; it is just that she listens to her emotions as well as using her intellect.

When Joe seems disturbed after the accident, his behaviour is particularly threatening for Clarissa because of her previous experience of madness in the family. It seems ironic that despite this she fails to recognize how dangerous Parry's behaviour is and misjudges Joe's.

Jed Parry

Again, we learn little about Parry's appearance other than from a few brief descriptions. Look at the first paragraph at the top of p. 24, Chapter 2, beginning *He was tall and lean ....*
❍ What are your first impressions of him? What do you think of Parry's habit of turning statements into questions? Is Joe right to be so critical of this habit of speech?

Parry's persistence about praying with Joe gives a hint of things to come. He does not take 'no' for an answer, trying a number of different approaches to persuade Joe. ❍ Given how events develop, is there anything Joe could have done to put Parry off?

The short description of Parry's footwear early in the novel is also important, because it gives us the first suggestion that he is following Joe in Chapter 4. *All I saw was a flash of a white shoe and something red.* That suggestion is vague enough for Clarissa to think that Joe is paranoid, because he did not exactly see Parry, just guessed that it must be him.

Parry's illness does not make him less intelligent or calculating, just obsessed. He hides his tracks cleverly. It cannot be a coincidence that Clarissa never actually sees him, and this makes it more difficult for her to believe Joe. Similarly, Parry is careful not to make direct threats, thus making Joe more vulnerable. The police think Joe is overreacting and refuse to give him their protection. Parry is also protected by money. Now that he has the inheritance he can afford to pay people for doing his dirty work. Some critics have expressed disbelief at the restaurant shooting. Surely Parry could have arranged the killing in Joe and Clarissa's apartment? On the other hand, it might be argued that an intense person like Parry would enjoy the drama of a public assassination. He might see it as a fitting punishment for Joe.

Although McEwan plays with the boundaries of abnormal and normal behaviour, we are left in no doubt of Parry's illness. There are elements of the young man's behaviour that remind us of someone madly in love rather than just mad, but it is also clear that he is unwell. Joe emphasizes Parry's instability in several ways. One of the most important is the description of his mood changes. *What was so exhausting about him was the variety of his emotional states and the speed of their transitions.* Then there is the suggestion that he hears voices. *He caught your eye, then turned his head to speak as though addressing a presence at his side, or an invisible creature perched on his shoulder.* Parry also speaks of 'signs', believing that Joe has left invisible messages in the curtains and bushes.

Interestingly, one of the most confusing things for Joe is the familiarity of Parry's 'routine'. He is unable to challenge Parry properly. *It took an act of will to dismiss the sense that I owed this man, that I was being unreasonable … In part, I was playing along with this domestic drama.* Parry uses the emotional vocabulary that a rejected lover might use and its familiar phrases catch Joe off balance. It is the odd combination of the familiar with unpredictable behaviour that causes so many problems.

Another difficulty for Joe is Parry's apparent vulnerability. At first, Joe cannot believe that Parry is harmful because he seems so pathetic. *He was a harmless fellow … he looked a sorry sight now … I had translated farce into indefinable menace.*

Most important is the destruction created by Parry. Not only does his illness create problems between Joe and Clarissa, the first few encounters between the two men churn up old insecurities in Joe about his career. *In my bad moments the thought returns that I'm a parasite … I sat again in my study, not working but brooding … my thoughts returned to how I came to be what I was, and how it might have been different.* Jed's particular type of illness makes him a catalyst in the lives of Joe and Clarissa. (A catalyst causes a change in things or people, rather like a chemical that makes other ingredients act differently when they are added together. Importantly, a catalyst does not change in the process of changing other things. ❷ How does this fit in with Jed's character and actions?) Jed sows the seeds of doubt and fear in his victims. Most importantly, he plans the shooting in the restaurant, almost killing a man. Finally, he endangers Clarissa's life.

Minor characters

RESCUERS

John Logan, 42, is a family doctor, husband and father of two children. He dies trying to save Harry Gadd from the balloon. **Joseph Lacey** is a farm labourer aged 63. He assists Joe in helping Jean Logan, by contacting James Reid and Bonnie Deedes. **Toby Greene** is a farm labourer aged 58.

JAMES AND HARRY GADD

James, aged 55, is a businessman and owner of the air balloon. His disregard for safety rules is partly responsible for the balloon getting out of control. **Harry** is his ten-year-old grandson whom John Logan dies trying to save.

FRIENDS AND A COLLEAGUE

Tom and Anna are friends of Joe and Clarissa. They listen to the couple pouring out their story on the night of the accident. **Eric** is a radio producer to whom Joe blurts out the story of the accident. He is embarrassed by Joe's behaviour.

JEAN LOGAN AND HER CHILDREN

Jean Logan is a historian, and the widow of John Logan. She is bitter and unable to grieve properly for her husband because she believes that he was having an affair. Their daughter **Rachael**, about ten years old, is concerned about her mother's behaviour. She is an intelligent girl who misses her father, so latches on to Joe, who is kind to her. Her brother **Leo**, aged about seven, is a friendly boy with a strong sense of right and wrong. The two children have a lot to teach the adults about love and forgiveness.

POLICE OFFICERS

Detective Inspector Linley is the first policeman to whom Joe speaks directly. He is dismissive about Joe's fears and patronizes him. **Detective Constable Wallace** is the police officer supervising the statements after the restaurant shooting. Like Linley, he does not believe Joe's story. Instead, he recommends antidepressants!

JOCELYN KALE

Probably in his sixties, Kale is godfather to Clarissa, as well as being an important scientist. He is present during the restaurant shoot-out.

COLIN TAPP

A government minister. Parry's hit men shoot him in the restaurant mistaking him for Joe, but he recovers.

JOHN WELLS (JOHNNY B)

An idealistic 'old hippie' drug-dealing friend from Joe's past. He helps Joe to find a gun for self-protection.

THE THREE GUN-SELLERS

Steve is the first of the trio. The three housemates are ex-criminals and failed property dealers, but all regard themselves as speakers of truth and hold many 'cosmic' ideas. Steve has an aggressive manner and provokes **Xan**, who almost kills Steve in a fight over the gun money. Unlike the two men, **Daisy** is unaggressive and takes the role of earth mother to the strange household. Nonetheless, she plays fair by making sure that Joe gets the gun before he leaves to escape the fight.

Test yourself

? Copy the Mini Mind Map at the beginning of the chapter. Add to it from memory. Then compare your completed Mind Map with the one opposite.
? Imagine that you are Clarissa. Make a 'for' and 'against' list of points as to whether she should stay in the relationship with Joe.

Now that you know who's who and who does what, it's time for a change. Take a short break before focusing on themes and ideas.

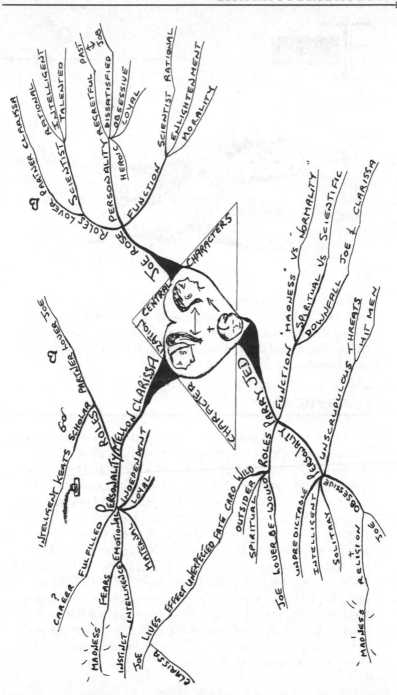

THEMES

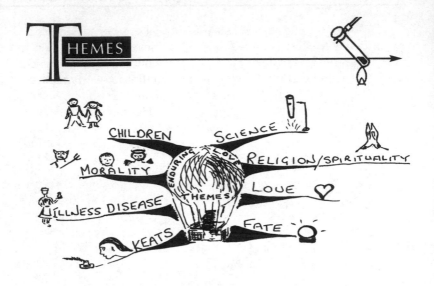

A **theme** is an idea which runs through a work and which is explored and developed along the way. The Mini Mind Map above shows the main themes of *Enduring Love*. Test yourself by copying it and then trying to add to it before comparing your results with the version on p. 25.

Science

Ian McEwan is fascinated by science and its impact upon our lives. Modern life would be much more difficult and dangerous without the advances that science and technology have brought. Of course, science in itself is not the cure to human problems; unscrupulous individuals and governments can use it for bad as well as good. For example, some people argue that a much larger proportion of science funding goes to weapons research than towards eradicating famine and illness. War is big business, yet many poor people are unable to afford basic medical treatment. However, most people would not like to go back to the harsh conditions of the past, even though they may wish that we could have more say in what kinds of science are funded and what it is used for. It is possible to criticize the way science is used yet be filled with wonder at some of its achievements!

Although some critics dislike the novel's use of science as a theme, McEwan has said that the achievements of science and scientific researchers 'rank with the work of Shakespeare, or the painting of the Sistine Chapel'. He finds it worrying that people who value the *life of the mind* and consider themselves intelligent beings can ignore science. He describes them as living *with one eye shut to that great triumph.* ✪ What do you think? Is the novel spoiled by scientific ideas, or do you think McEwan is right?

Joe is a rational man whose work involves explaining science to ordinary people. His scientific training makes him sceptical of anything that cannot be proven. Jed Parry on the other hand, has a mystical view of the world. He believes in a guiding, conscious force – God – that is responsible for everything. Throughout the novel, ideas about the rational and spiritual are debated. Clarissa may also be said to represent the instinctual, emotional world, in that she is an expert on Keats, one of the Romantic poets. (See 'Context' for more on the Romantics.) However, perhaps Clarissa represents the more acceptable side of such ways of describing the world because she is emotionally stable and her job analyses literature in an intellectual way. Yet Joe is also capable of self-questioning. Remind yourself of his attempts in Chapter 5 to prove the influence of traditional narrative on nineteenth-century scientific writing. Eventually he is honest enough to admit that his evidence is flawed. In contrast, Parry disregards anything that does not fit into his world-view.

Religion and spirituality

Roughly speaking, religion tends to be focused on a particular god or gods with a definite set of beliefs and rules, whereas spirituality is a looser belief in the spirit or in the powers of nature or the occult – things that we cannot prove with science at present. Believing in something outside so-called normal, everyday existence is important to many people in the world because it helps them cope with the big questions about life and death. Many human beings want spiritual comfort because the world can seem like a frightening place without a god figure. Studying the lives of holy men and women can be inspiring. Organized religion and other spiritual ideas give us a set of moral rules by which to live our lives. They also give a framework to the feelings of wonder and awe we feel about nature and the universe.

However, those without such beliefs, like atheists and humanists, believe that we can appreciate the wonders of life without believing in unproved theories. Moreover, many would argue that religion in particular is capable of allowing intolerance and cruelty, such as that of the Spanish Inquisition. Throughout human history, terrible wars and atrocities have occurred in the name of religion. For instance, quotations from the Old Testament were once used to justify the slavery of black people. Even today, most religions condemn sexual relationships that do not take the traditional form of marriage, even though many people no longer want to get married.

McEwan is not trying to argue a simple 'right and wrong' approach to life, that science is more important than the spiritual or the other way round. Instead, he shows the drawbacks of a rigid approach. Jed Parry's religious beliefs are dogmatic to the point of insanity. Yet there are moments of joy in his life that are hard to ignore. Similarly, Joe's rational approach sometimes misses out on instinctive, 'gut' feelings. On the surface, Clarissa seems to have the balance right – but nonetheless gets it wrong about Parry and Joe's 'madness'.

Ironically, Joe may be said to find some sort of spirituality in his relationship with Clarissa, although he would probably deny this. For example, in Chapter 3, he uses spiritual language such as *blessed, deliverance, forgive* and *absolving* to describe the comfort they give each other after the accident. For many people, romantic love is the nearest to a godly experience they ever get.

Love

The title of the novel is *Enduring Love*, after all! The most dramatic example of love in the novel is that of Jed for Joe. As one critic remarked, the most disturbing aspect of Parry's illness is how close it often seems to ordinary romantic feelings. That is ironic, because we live in a society that encourages us to look for true, lasting love, but this particular 'enduring love' is both dangerous and hopeless.

The other important love is that between Joe and Clarissa. Their relationship is threatened by Jed's obsession and there comes a point when we doubt whether it will survive. However, it does 'endure'; we discover at the end of the novel not only that they are reconciled, but also that they adopt a child.

Love of children is the third sort of love. The tragedy of the Logan children losing their father, and Clarissa's inability to bear children even though she desperately wants them, are important issues in the novel. Indeed, it is the Logan children who symbolize the hope of reconciliation between Joe and Clarissa in Chapter 24.

Fate

From the novel's opening chapter, the randomness of fate is a recurring theme. If Joe and Clarissa had not been present at the accident, if Joe had not caught Jed's eye ... . Even Joe's rational nature cannot prepare him for the unpredictable series of events that changes his life for ever. Although science seems to be about finding patterns so that we can understand our world and universe, recent research on Chaos theory suggests that many things are 'random' and unpredictable.

Keats the poet

Keats' ideas form part of the novel's framework. They are dealt with in more detail in the 'Context' section. In addition to the links with Clarissa, whose career is based on the study of his works, Keats' life suggests some parallels with that of Jed Parry. Both men lost their mothers when relatively young. Parry feels rejected by Joe in the way Keats supposedly did by the woman he loved, Fanny Brawne, and also by his hero, the poet Wordsworth. Keats came from quite humble origins, as does Parry, who has only recently – and unexpectedly – inherited his wealth. Keats' illness shortened his life and prevented him from marrying Fanny, whereas Parry's mental illness stops him from having a normal relationship. The two men also suffer from unrequited love.

Parry does not die young like Keats, but his imprisonment in a psychiatric hospital prevents him from living his life in the usual way. Finally, Keats had a spiritual approach to life that might be compared to Parry's, although there are differences – mainly, that the poet lived a relatively peaceful and blameless life.

Disease and illness

The most obvious representation of this theme is Parry's mental illness, but there are also other references. Joe refers to *the sickness of guilt* after the accident and feels like *the bearer ... of a freshly mutated virus of misfortune.* In addition, the effects of Parry's love on Joe and Clarissa might be compared to an infectious disease that destroys everything in its path.

McEwan seems to be making us question our ideas about mental illness in particular. The line between sanity and madness is shown to be a thin one when even calm, rational Joe responds to his situation in ways that seem strange to Clarissa and the police.

Morality

Ideas of right and wrong are debated throughout the novel. Religious people usually have a clear set of rules, but Joe is a good-living atheist who has his own code of behaviour. However, Jed and Joe both behave in ways that many would believe are 'wrong'. Jed hires men to kill Joe, whereas Joe has taken illegal drugs in his youth and buys a gun from known criminals. Morality is hard to pin down in the novel. Was Logan a hero or an irresponsible fool who condemned his children and wife to unhappiness? Who first let go of the balloon rope and was that person truly responsible for Logan's death? Are human beings naturally selfish or naturally co-operative? Similarly, the three hippies are desperate for the money from the gun but want to feel guilt-free about the consequences of its use.

Then again, is killing always wrong? What about killing to defend your family or country? What would happen to society if everyone behaved like Joe and shot at people who threatened them? Even the Logan children become involved in a discussion about 'moral relativism' in Chapter 14.

○ Think about your own moral dilemmas. What if you buy products, such as trainers or chocolate, that result in terrible poverty, illness or early death for the workers who make them? Are you responsible in some way? McEwan emphasizes the moral maze of modern life, in which traditional teachings about right and wrong are often under question.

Children

Children are our link between the past and the future. We often get compared to older or even dead relatives when young. Children represent hope for the future, the continuation of the family line.

The opening chapter features the attempted rescue of a boy from an air balloon. A young child in danger is an emotive subject and therefore an effective opening for a story. Later on, Clarissa is distressed by John Logan's death because he left two young children behind – she herself loves children but has been unable to have any. Joe says that she is *asking her own past, her ghost child to forgive her.* Ironically, the Logan children take a liking to Joe, treating him like a substitute father, and it is they who take his hand at the end of Chapter 24, as if to symbolize hope and continuity. John Logan is dead, but in a way he lives on in Rachael and Leo.

Parry also shows childlike qualities in his desperate search for love. Although claiming that he is 'in love' with Joe, he seems quite sexless and is embarrassed when Joe mentions sex. The few references to his background in Chapter 11 hint at a sad, lonely childhood and youth. His father died when he was eight and his mother only four years before the novel opens. Perhaps he is looking for a father figure in Joe. He seems like an isolated, unloved young man and is quite friendless. His directness and lack of subtlety also hint at a childlike attitude to life.

Try this

? Look at the Mini Mind Map at the beginning of this chapter. Develop it with your own ideas. Compare your finished Mind Map with the one opposite.

? Write key sentences summarizing the importance of each theme.

? Write the keywords of each theme on a large sheet of paper. Choose two themes and draw a line between them. Explain how they are connected.

Now you know the main themes, take a break.

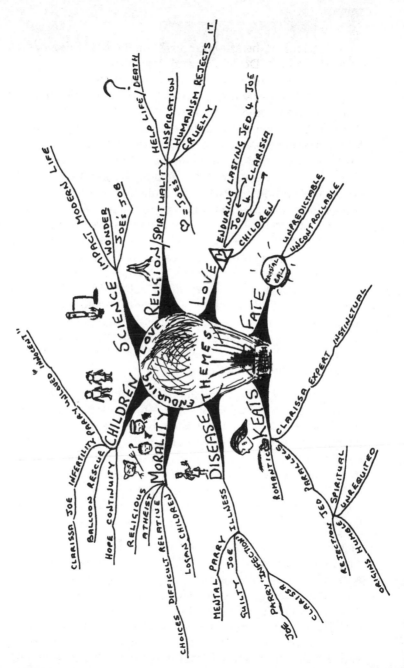

LANGUAGE, STYLE AND STRUCTURE

McEwan subverts the thriller genre – in other words, he plays around with the 'rules' of this sort of story. The novel resembles a thriller at first glance. A fatal accident provokes a disturbed young man into stalking a complete stranger. Jed pays hired assassins to murder Joe, and then Joe rescues Clarissa, who is being held at knifepoint by Jed. However, the novel goes further than the usual thriller, in that it isn't all action. Joe is a thinker, an 'ideas person' who has to review his own life after the balloon accident changes everything he once took for granted. Throughout the novel we are presented with intellectual discussions on topics such as humanity's place in the universe, Keats' poetry, religion, science – all of which are meant to make us think more deeply about life. The novel is also more obviously literary than many conventional action novels because it pays special attention to language and theme. (Having said that, many modern thrillers are recognized as literature and also deal with the difficult business of being human!)

The author plays with conventional narrative ('ordinary' storytelling techniques). Firstly, the novel is written in the form of a fictional character, Joe, writing in the first person. McEwan changes this occasionally by giving Parry a voice in some chapters and by Joe writing from Clarissa's point of view, but in the third person, in another chapter. Then there is a note from Clarissa to Joe near the end of the novel. The novel also jumps around in time. Joe often daydreams or speculates in the middle of an episode, interrupting the action.

In addition, there is fake 'non-fiction' medical writing in Appendix I that plays with our ideas about authority in writing. Appendix I is an 'official' version of events and seems to verify Joe's story, although of course it, too, is partly fiction because it deals with Jed's illness and behaviour towards Joe and Clarissa. In fact we have no way of being sure if even the introduction is genuine unless we research whether there is such a publication and whether it featured the article on de

Clérambault's syndrome! ✪ Why has McEwan used this format? Is it because Joe is an **unreliable narrator** (one whose knowledge and judgements are limited and biased)? After all, we have been given hints about that by Clarissa's narratives, in which she complains of his secrecy, his dishonesty and his one-sided approach to the crisis with Jed Parry. Or is Joe trying to emphasize that he was right about Parry all along?

The mixture of differing viewpoints and written styles in the novel is quite typical of modern literature. Finally, you may wish to ask yourself why Joe's viewpoint is the dominant one in the novel. ✪ Imagine the novel written from Clarissa's point of view, or Jean Logan's – or even Jed Parry's! How would they regard the events, do you think, and how would this affect our reactions as readers?

Setting

Places in *Enduring Love* often have symbolic and thematic significance. The significance of each of the main settings, the countryside, London and the Logans' house, is outlined below.

THE COUNTRYSIDE

The main part of the novel begins and ends in the countryside. Natural surroundings often suggest a safe and beautiful escape from modern urban life, but in *Enduring Love* the innocence and joy of the picnic are shattered by tragedy and the countryside takes on a sinister aspect. It is as if Joe and Clarissa are Adam and Eve thrown out of their happy life – the Garden of Eden – into doubt and despair. Despite the natural beauty of their surroundings, the wind is dangerous and contributes to the balloon accident. McEwan presents the other side of nature, one that is life-threatening and unpredictable.

In Chapter 24, most of the central characters return to the countryside. This time it is a place of forgiveness and new beginnings. No longer threatening, nature is a place of peace and comfort and the river a hopeful symbol of life and change. The use of a similar setting at the beginning and end of the novel is the closest McEwan brings us to a happy ending. There are still loose ends to the story, but using the countryside setting as 'bookends' at the start and finish gives the sense that all the characters have at least some chance of moving on and finding a new life. The only exception to that is Jed Parry, whose illness prevents him from accepting change.

LONDON

This is where Joe feels most at home. His emotional and work life is based in the big city. He seems to like living there, but it becomes a place of danger once Parry starts to pursue him. He is not safe anywhere, not even in a large, busy restaurant.

THE SUBURBS

Joe and Johnny B drive to the suburbs to buy the gun. Many people move out of the city to escape the noise and pollution, but the suburban home of the three hippies is not exactly a haven. Ironically, Johnny comments 'it's good to get out of the city,' but the place where the hippies live is ramshackle and Steve and Xan quarrel violently. Joe is out of his element here, and not only because of the danger involved in buying a gun. There are big class and education differences between him and the others. He is a well-educated, prosperous and sophisticated Londoner, whereas they are failed criminals with few social skills. He does not fit in here, just as he feels out of place in Jean Logan's middle-class but uncomfortable house in Oxford.

Get stylish!

? Make a chart of the main events in the novel.
? Make a Mind Map of the three types of settings, adding quotations if you can.

Time for a short break ...

Section 1, Chapters 1–3
The accident and its aftermath

Chapter 1 *A terrible thing*

◆ Joe Rose, the narrator, describes events prior to a tragic accident.
◆ He backtracks to earlier in the day.
◆ Whilst picnicking, the couple hear a man's cry for help then run to the rescue.
◆ Six men try to rescue a boy from an air balloon.
◆ The wind forces all except James Logan to let go. He hangs on and falls to his death.

The beginning is simple to mark, gives the novel a sharp opening sentence, as well as suggesting that what follows is difficult. Everything before the accident is a reminder of how safe and predictable life once was, yet Joe also describes it as *the pinprick on the time map*, reminding us of its insignificance when compared to the enormous upheavals throughout the universe's history. There is some truth in this, but it is also typical of Joe's tendency to be over-analytical.

The chapter moves between nostalgia for the past before the accident, and sorrow and fear for the future. Joe tells himself off for returning to the scene in his memory: *what idiocy, to be racing into this story and its labyrinths, sprinting away from our happiness*. The verbs *racing* and *sprinting* emphasize the speed of events over which they have no control.

Clarissa has just returned from a long research trip abroad. Joe buys picnic food to celebrate. Their enjoyment of the countryside on a beautiful spring day acts as a strong contrast to the death of Logan at the end of the chapter. Despite their happiness, we learn about some crucial differences between the couple. Joe is very analytical and Clarissa teases him by calling him *the world's most complicated simpleton*. This is the first hint that their differences may create difficulties for them later.

? Morality concerns standards of right and wrong. The letting go of the balloon ropes (causing Logan's death) makes Joe think deeply about human behaviour. As he explains, human survival depended on co-operation until relatively recently. In contrast, there is individual selfishness. *Treading that line, keeping the others in check and being kept in check by them, is what we call morality ... mostly, we are good when it makes sense.* ❂ Do you agree with Joe here? Or do you think he is being cynical? What about people who risk their lives or careers to do 'the right thing'?

Look at the use of scientific and mathematical metaphors. Before Logan's death Joe refers to a *comforting geometry* and *the knowable, limited plane of the snooker table* when describing the fields around them. In contrast, the way that everyone is drawn into the accident is compared to *the power of a terrible ratio*. The accident itself is described as *a kind of furnace in whose heat identities and fates would buckle into new shapes*. Science and mathematics can be comforting when they help humans to control and understand the world, but can also remind us of our helplessness.

Keats the poet is mentioned for the first time in this chapter. Clarissa has been hunting for some missing letters written by him. Indeed, letters feature frequently in the novel – Parry pesters Joe with letters and Clarissa writes a letter asking Joe for a trial separation. Ironically, Clarissa wants Keats' letters but fails to find them, just before Joe is bombarded with unwanted communication from Parry. Remember also that Keats was in love with a woman (Fanny Brawne) but was doomed never to marry her, rather like Parry and his hopeless love for Joe.

The sense of fate is strong throughout the chapter, yet it is written from hindsight. *This was the moment ... at that moment.* Had Clarissa and Joe been able to predict what would happen they could have avoided it. It is fate, or a series of strange coincidences, that makes events turn out the way that they do.

LANGUAGE, STYLE AND STRUCTURE

Joe refers to a buzzard circling overhead, hinting at the disaster to come. Remember that buzzards are birds of prey. It may also symbolize Joe's scientific detachment – looking, but not emotionally involved.

McEwan uses personification to show the wind as a powerful force against which humans have no control. *The wind renewed its rage … a mighty fist socked the balloon in two rapid blows, one-two.* ○ What sort of human (and sport!) does this description suggest?

The entire chapter is written to convey the adrenaline rush of fear. It leaps between calm descriptions of the picnic scene then jumps back and forward in time, rather like someone rushing about in panic. It also includes dramatic, tension-filled phrases such as: *the encounter that would unhinge us was minutes away … a whole stage of my life closed.* ○ Can you find any more examples that convey this atmosphere?

Joe refers to the Fall, meaning the Adam and Eve story in the Old Testament. According to the tale, the first humans lived in a state of happy innocence (grace) until they disobeyed God. They were punished by being expelled from Paradise, also known as the Garden of Eden. Many major religions use the story to explain human unhappiness and wickedness. Many writers have used the Fall as a symbolic device. In McEwan's novel it is Logan's literal fall from a balloon that causes a 'fall from grace' for so many of the witnesses because it ruins their lives.

When Logan falls he does so because everyone else lets go. As well as referring to human selfishness, some critics have suggested that this may also be a metaphor for love. If one person in a relationship loses their trust, or 'lets go', then the relationship is doomed to failure. ○ If you have already read the novel, think about how this metaphor relates to Joe and Clarissa. If you have not, perhaps you could come back to this idea later.

'Selfishness is also written on our hearts.'

Chapter 2 *'God has brought us together'*

◆ Joe is in shock after Logan's death. He becomes manic.

◆ Joe goes to inspect Logan's body. Parry follows, then begs him to pray; Joe refuses.

◆ Joe notices that Parry seems rather odd.

The chapter begins as if Joe is thinking aloud: *best to slow down.* He reminds himself that he does not have to imitate the speed of the actual events, but should describe everything carefully. He also realizes that it is difficult to pin down the actual 'moment of truth': *there are always antecedent causes.* (*Antecedent* means 'prior', 'happening before'.)

Gradually it becomes apparent that Joe's reactions are dulled. Firstly, he is aware of Clarissa's tears, but comments that *to me, sorrow seemed a long way off.* He describes himself as if he is in an old dream. *My emotional responses were non-existent or inappropriate.* Shock makes people react in different ways, but it is typical of the couple that Joe switches off emotionally, whereas Clarissa does not.

He watches himself 'perform'. *I was in a soap opera.* The shock has made him manic and emotionally detached. Clarissa tries to calm him but he is too far-gone to understand. It is not until his walk towards Logan's body that he begins to return to normal. Fear and dread kick in instead.

Look at the first encounter between Joe and Jed Parry. Joe is self-assured at this point. He is critical of Parry's tone of voice. *Parry had his generation's habit of making a statement on the rising inflection of a question.* In other words, the younger man's voice rises at the end of sentences so that he sounds as if he is asking questions instead of making statements. ✪ Do you ever speak in this way, or do you know anyone who does? Are Joe's criticisms of this way of speaking fair or not?

Joe describes Parry's behaviour from hindsight. *He was excited, but no one could ever have guessed to what extent.* ✪ Do you think anything that Joe could have said or done would have prevented Parry from fixating on him?

The role of fate is re-emphasized. *So much followed from this incident, so much branching and subdivision began in those early moments ... the explosion of consequences.*

Whole books ... are dedicated to the first half-minute in the history of the universe. Vertiginous (dizzying) theories of chaos and turbulence are predicated upon the supremacy of initial conditions which need painstaking depiction. In other words, huge upheavals in the universe's creation might only take seconds, but these must be studied and explained thoroughly if we are to understand them properly. Joe's scientific training tells him to think logically and carefully, even though his gut instinct is to spill it all out in a rush.

Seeing the dead man makes Joe think about the reasons for religion. *There was no one there ... a pre-scientific age would have needed to invent the soul.* It is not just the terrible damage to Logan's body that convinces Joe of the death. It is Logan's *absence* that makes death so shocking – the body remains but the energy that made that person alive is no longer there. Religion believes in life after death, that the soul or spirit of the dead person goes elsewhere. There is no solid proof and science tells us that death is the end of life as we know it. Nonetheless, Joe accepts that however logical we are, *fear and awe still surprise us in the presence of the dead.*

Parry invites Joe to pray with him beside Logan's body. Joe politely refuses, but Parry persists. Joe finally says: *'No one's listening. There's no one up there.'* ✪ Why does this remark make Parry smile so joyously? What does this tell us about him in hindsight?

There are religious echoes in the final sentence of the chapter. Joe thinks that the arrival of the police has rescued him from *the radiating power of Jed Parry's love and pity.* As well as making Parry sound Christ-like, this is ironic because the effects of his behaviour will 'radiate' or spread further than Joe could ever imagine. Indeed, the police fail to 'rescue' him until the very end of the novel.

When Joe makes the decision to run towards the balloon, he says he *chose a branching in the paths that foreclosed a certain kind of easeful life.* The phrase *easeful life* is a reference to a famous Keats poem called 'Ode to a Nightingale' although the original was written as 'half in love with easeful death'. 'Easeful' is an old word that means (roughly) free from pain or worry. Joe thinks he is heading for a pleasant middle age, but the events of one afternoon change all that. In the original, the poet thinks romantically that it might be no bad thing to die whilst listening to the 'ecstasy' of the nightingale's beautiful song. Joe's situation is brutal and leaves him no room for imagination. His life is threatened by a stalker and he longs for life, not death.

LANGUAGE, STYLE AND STRUCTURE

I was in the world, equipped, capable, connected. Joe reels off a list of adjectives that make him appear in control. The sentence is clipped and efficient-sounding, but hints at his manic state.

Later in the chapter, the slow build-up creates suspense before Joe reaches the dead man. McEwan takes about a page to describe Joe's walk. Logan looks so normal from the back that Joe makes us wonder if he is still alive.

Chapter 3 *The sickness of guilt*

◆ Joe and Clarissa return home and try to make sense of the tragedy.
◆ Clarissa sympathizes with the Logan children.
◆ She wants to believe that Logan died for a reason.
◆ She and Joe make love, which helps to take away the shadow of death.
◆ Joe gets a phone call from Parry. He recognizes the voice, but lies to Clarissa about it: *a serious mistake.*

Shock and grief pass through different stages as we try to come to terms with a disturbing event. Joe and Clarissa are no different, even though they are fictional characters. When they return home, their relief turns to guilt. How can things seem so normal when they have just watched a man die? McEwan uses dramatic words such as *torrent, post-mortem, exorcism* to emphasize the intensity of their talk.

They can do nothing but go over the accident repeatedly. They keep backing off from the actual moment of death yet return to it despite their reluctance.

While Clarissa struggles to understand Logan's death, Joe worries that she is trying to give some spiritual meaning to the tragedy. As an atheist, he believes that Logan's death was pointless, like so many deaths, but Clarissa explains that she is just trying to make sense of it. She teases Joe for being *'such a dope'*, then adds *'you're so rational sometimes you're like a child'*. Their differences are not yet a problem but will become so later in the novel. Joe over-intellectualizes things, whereas Clarissa uses her emotions as well as her intellect. She laughs about Joe's strange behaviour after the death: *'I love you more now I've seen you go completely mad … the rationalist cracks at last!'* Joe jokes, *'it's just the beginning … stick around.'* In fact, this comment foreshadows the future, when Joe becomes so disturbed by Jed Parry that Clarissa really does worry that he has gone mad.

Talking about their past experiences of fear is a way of coming to terms with what they feel now. Their lovemaking is comforting and helps them to sleep. Friends visit later and they talk late into the night. The couple are asleep when Parry rings. Joe is surprised but instead of telling Clarissa, he lies. ❂ Why doesn't he tell Clarissa the truth? Why is this such a problem later in the novel?

Joe is an atheist, but he uses many spiritual metaphors in this chapter. Expressions such as *ritual* and *incantations* describe the way he and Clarissa go over and over the details of the accident, as if they are chanting or praying. He uses *blessed, ecstasy* and their *absolving* (releasing from blame) to describe the comfort they give each other. Their union gives them *deliverance*, as if they are 'saved'.

As was mentioned in the commentary on Chapter 1, the use of the word *fall* has religious associations, as well as its literal meaning. Clarissa refers to Milton's work *Paradise Lost*, which is based on the story of the Fall. At the fatal moment that Logan fell, Clarissa hoped for a good angel to fly down and rescue him. She does not really believe in such things, it is just an expression of hope against despair. Such images form part of her imagination because she has studied literature for most of her life.

We learn that Clarissa cannot bear children. This has been a terrible sorrow for her because she loves children, but she uses her maternal instincts on the children of family and friends. Joe recounts her *disabling grief* over the death of a friend's young baby. He believes that she was *mourning for a phantom child* – the child she dreamed of but was unable to bear. Clarissa also identifies with Logan because he died and left his own children fatherless while trying to save another child's life. We are reminded of the Logan orphans when Joe imagines them as *two baffled children* not understanding why a policeman has come to their house. It is a brief but moving mention of what the tragedy will mean to Logan's family.

LANGUAGE, STYLE AND STRUCTURE

McEwan uses striking metaphors to describe the couple's attempts to avoid mentioning Logan's death. *We backed away … circling it, stalking it, until we had it cornered and began to tame it with words.* He makes the death sound like a dangerous animal that they are trying to control. Another phrase describes the *knots, tangles of horror.* They feel like *prisoners in a cell … our prison grew larger.* Death is one of the last big taboos, and many cultures avoid talking about death directly. This is why we often use euphemisms such as 'passed away'.

Later, Joe compares them to *dedicated craftsmen at work, grinding the jagged edge of memories,* as if they are trying to smooth rough metal.

Test yourself

(Answers at end of Commentary)

? (a) How would you describe the style of Chapter 1?
 (b) What is 'the Fall'?
 (c) Why does John Logan die – in Joe's opinion?
 (d) What upsets Clarissa most about the accident?
 (e) Who phones Joe in the early hours? What does Joe say to Clarissa and why is it important later in the novel?

? What are your opinions of Joe as a partner/husband so far? Make a Mini Mind Map and do the same for Clarissa.

? Underline the words and phrases that you think apply to Jed Parry's behaviour in Chapter 2: religious; friendly; sensitive; eccentric; obsessive; unsure; forceful; cynical; lonely; insensitive.

Tragedy, shock and lives turned upside down: take a break before discovering how the accident affects Joe Rose – and Jed Parry.

Section 2, Chapters 4–8
The stalking begins

Chapter 4 *The unnamed sensation*

◆ Clarissa and Joe return to work.
◆ Joe writes about the Hubble telescope. He feels uneasy throughout the day.
◆ He embarrasses a producer by talking too much about the accident.
◆ He later begins an article about narrative writing in science.
◆ Joe realizes that his unease is fear. He half senses that he is being watched.

The routine of work is welcome to the couple after the distress of the accident. Joe works at home on the Hubble article. He begins to feel uneasy but cannot put a label on his feelings. *A physical sensation that I could not quite identify.* He does not believe that this feeling is guilt.

Joe is still disturbed by the accident, as we can see from the way he rants at the producer about it. As he humorously admits, it could have been anyone: *a goldfish would have served me as well as a talks producer.* The other man is desperate to get away, which shows how embarrassing Joe is being.

After the meeting, he visits a library and researches the history of scientific writing. Although soothed by the peaceful atmosphere, he becomes aware of intrusive footsteps. He sees someone leave out of the corner of his eye. *At that stage I still had not grasped the promptings of footwear and colour.* He finally understands that his uneasiness is actually fear and rushes out to find the owner of the white trainers and red laces that he saw leaving. ✪ Who does he think he has seen? Note the ominous hint of trouble when Joe mentions Yvonne Fletcher, the police officer who was shot by terrorists.

In this chapter we see Joe's gut instincts fighting to come through. Unpredictable emotions can be seen in his talk with the producer and also his feelings of unease. His intellect tries to ignore such feelings by focusing on ideas and writing, but he is unable to do so.

A brief mention of marital problems between Clarissa's brother and sister-in-law acts as a foreshadowing of the problems that Joe and Clarissa will experience later.

The Hubble telescope is an interesting topic for Joe to write about at this time because it represents failure. The telescope was a noble gesture that at first went badly wrong – a bit like Logan's sacrifice, perhaps. Joe also has feelings of failure about his lack of achievement in scientific research.

The second reference to science is in Joe's research on methods of scientific writing. The nineteenth-century example of the dog and its master is a good one. The writer's subjective style means that the dog is credited with human emotions that it does not have. Joe also gets irritated with the lack of scientific books in the library, rather like McEwan's own opinion. *Did the scientific illiterates who ran this place ... really believe that literature was the greatest intellectual achievement of our civilization?* The use of a rhetorical question emphasizes his exasperation.

When Joe tells Eric the producer about the accident, he describes him as *looking at me as though I were contaminated, the bearer ... of a freshly mutated virus of ill-fortune.* The bearer of bad news is often resented. ✪ Why do you think this is? Is it some primitive feeling that we might 'catch' bad luck like we catch a virus, or do we just hate being reminded that we will die someday?

Joe rearranges a jam jar full of flowers that have been knocked over. Despite his atheism, he hopes the gesture might bring him luck and realizes that *on such hopeful acts of propitiation ... whole religions were founded.* In other words, humans try to prevent terrible, unpredictable things happening to them by performing ceremonies to keep the gods happy.

LANGUAGE, STYLE AND STRUCTURE

McEwan uses words associated with dirtiness to suggest Joe's unease. *It was like the sensation of not having washed ... I felt tainted ... unclean, contaminated ....* The feelings are so strong that they are physical as well as psychological.

Chapter 5 *Someone at my back*

◆ Joe returns home in an agitated state. He now believes Parry was following him.
◆ Joe works in order to calm himself.
◆ Clarissa arrives home after an unsettling meeting with her brother. She and Joe comfort each other.
◆ Joe decides not to disturb their peace by mentioning Parry.

Joe is desperate to talk to Clarissa about Parry, but she is out, so he tries to distract himself with television. Despite its horrors, the familiarity of the news and weather coverage soothes him. He compares it to an *opiate* (a mind-numbing drug).

Although he is sure that it was Parry following him he has no real proof. He uses last number recall to confirm that the phone call was from Parry, then begins to worry about what the man wants from him.

Work gives Joe an escape from his fears, so he drifts into the *desired state, the high-walled prison of infinite thought.* He writes more about the effect of narrative in science before giving it up. Clarissa returns home and they seek comfort in each other's arms. It is this that stops Joe from telling Clarissa about Jed Parry. *All urgency had gone.* Nonetheless, the fact that Joe asks rhetorical questions on the last page suggests that he is questioning his decision in hindsight. *Would it have been right then ... to intrude upon our happiness? ... could I have destroyed our tenderness...?*

Joe has a hypothesis, an idea: as the novel was the most important art form in the last century, perhaps its narrative style influenced scientific writing. After spending several hours on research, he realizes that he has no firm evidence. He has simply been twisting a few 'facts' to fit his hypothesis and is forced to admit the truth to himself. The incident is a subtle comparison with the way Jed Parry twists everything to fit his obsession with Joe. For all Joe's emotional clumsiness at times, he is a man who believes in honesty and truth.

The second reference to science concerns the fear response in human beings. Joe explains how our basic emotions are actually primitive chemical reactions in the body.

Joe thinks about the surprise that we feel when meeting up with loved ones again, despite knowing them so well. Although he is romantic about Clarissa, he turns to science for an explanation. Perhaps it helps love to last, so that we can produce children, or *genetic footprints* as he calls them.

LANGUAGE, STYLE AND STRUCTURE

Instead of using the traditional suspense mechanisms of the thriller, McEwan creates a diversion in our minds. When Joe hears something behind him – *there was someone at my back* – he immediately launches into an explanation about the fight and flight reaction in humans. After a paragraph of this, he returns to the actual event and describes his emotional reactions. This is typical of Joe, in that he often uses his intellect before opening up to an emotional response. Yet perhaps the author is also trying to suggest that we have more control of our feelings (such as fear) if we understand why they occur. McEwan's technique also leaves the reader in the dark for a while – is Joe in danger or not? So perhaps this is quite a sophisticated method of prolonging suspense!

Notice also the references to humans as creatures. As a scientist, Joe is aware of our place in the universe. Firstly, he reminds us that our fear responses come from a time when we had to avoid predators – dangerous creatures. He then mentions Clarissa's *animal presence*, meaning her presence as a purely physical being, not one of intellect. Later, he mentions the two of them leaving the pressure of everyday life. *We tumbled out of our respective days, like creatures shaken from a net.*

Chapter 6 *'But you didn't actually see him'*

◆ Joe wakes early, worried about his part in Logan's death.
◆ He tells Clarissa about Parry. She is concerned but cautious.
◆ Parry rings and Joe agrees to meet him.

We discover more about the life shared by Clarissa and Joe. They own a flat in Maida Vale, a middle-class area of West London. The apartment block is slightly shabby but pleasant. They have roof access, a detail that is important near the end of the novel.

Joe reflects on his part in Logan's death. The second big question he must think about is whether to visit Logan's widow or not. When Clarissa returns home he attempts to tell her about Jed Parry, but she finds it amusing. *'A secret gay love affair with a Jesus freak! I can't wait to tell your science friends.'* She is sceptical, pointing out that Joe did not actually see him and does not think the situation is serious. Joe feels reassured by her calmness.

As Clarissa leaves, however, Joe is startled by a phone call from Parry. Joe finally agrees to Parry's request to meet up: *'just see me this once.'* He is very shocked to realize that Parry is in the phone box next to Joe and Clarissa's home. Parry not only has their telephone number, he knows where they live. Joe hopes that he can put Parry off for good.

? Joe cannot work out who let go of the balloon rope first and he makes mathematical calculations as well as moral ones in his attempt to come to terms with the guilt. *How was it possible to tell Mrs Logan of her husband's sacrifice without drawing her attention to our own cowardice. Or, was it his folly?* He turns over the question in his mind. ✪ What do you think? Did Joe and the other men act selfishly or was it just a tragic accident that was beyond their control?

Joe and Clarissa seem to have swapped roles temporarily. Joe insists that it was Parry following him and explains that he knew something was wrong earlier in the day. *'It was just a feeling, a bad feeling.'* This time it is Clarissa who wants solid proof.

LANGUAGE, STYLE AND STRUCTURE

One of the supposed differences between 'popular' and 'literary' writing is that literature pays more attention to language and form. Certainly, McEwan uses some startling metaphors throughout this novel, as well as using different narrative forms. In this chapter alone, there are some striking images.

Firstly, the covering on the roof is described as *an elephant's hide*. McEwan also uses an oxymoron to describe the noise of the traffic: *tranquillising thunder*. In the next paragraph he refers to *blustery sunshine*. One meaning of 'bluster' is that of 'empty threats or protests'. ✪ Could this be a hint about Joe's guilt about the accident – is he trying to mentally 'bluster' his way out of responsibility and does he realize this deep down?

Later in the chapter, Clarissa is described as *moving through the conversation with the caution of a bomb disposal expert*. The powerful metaphor suggests that she is actually quite worried about Joe's state of mind.

Chapter 7 *'The purpose is to bring you to the Christ that is in you ...'*

- ◆ Jed Parry declares his love before accusing Joe of misusing his 'power' over him.
- ◆ Parry says the 'feeling' is there to bring Joe to God.
- ◆ He assumes that Joe will leave Clarissa for him.
- ◆ Joe escapes in a taxi, telling Parry to leave him alone.

Joe is struck by how harmless and pathetic Parry looks: *smaller, all knobs and bones ... a sorry sight.* Parry weeps because he believes that Joe is denying his real feelings in order to have more power. *'You don't have to do this to me.'* However much Joe insists that he is not interested, Parry will not accept rejection. The younger man's mood-changes worry Joe.

Parry insists that there was a religious moment after Logan's death. *'Something passed between us, up there on the hill, after he fell. It was pure energy, pure light?'* According to him, they are meant to be together so that Joe can find God. To Joe the atheist, this is meaningless, but he finds the conversation difficult. *What also amazed me was how easy it was not to say, 'Who the fuck are you? What are you talking about?'* Joe realizes that he is going along with Parry's reasoning because the emotional language is familiar and he feels himself slipping into a *domestic drama*. In hindsight, Joe swears in his mind at the outrageousness of Parry's demands, but is unable to challenge them openly at the time. The final straw is when Parry suggests that the three of them need to '*talk*'.

Joe is at a loss. Nothing from his rational approach to life can help him because he is confronted with Parry's absolute conviction that something meaningful has taken place between them. Parry simply interprets events in his way and accuses Joe of pretending not to understand.

The novel's title can be interpreted in different ways. 'Enduring', as an adjective, means 'lasting', but as a verb it means 'undergoing hardship or strain' – putting up with love! Parry's love is indeed lasting, but the experience is also like an endurance test for each man. It brings more pain than joy.

Chapter 8 *I'm in a relationship*

◆ Joe considers the 'intellectual revolution' – new theories about the origins of human behaviour.
◆ The police won't help.
◆ The pressure makes Joe brood about his career.
◆ Parry continues to stalk Joe.

Joe eventually dismisses the *confused and eccentric young man* from his thoughts, misguidedly believing him to be inadequate but harmless. Instead, he thinks about his latest article, the reasons why humans smile. It triggers the memory of a discussion that he once had with Clarissa about new scientific ideas. Joe suggested that she was over-influenced by Keats in her thinking about science. The poet believed that it was *robbing the world of wonder*. In contrast, Joe's opinion was that knowing more only increases our awareness of how miraculous life is. Clarissa argued that he had misunderstood her, saying that if we only analyse *the bits* that explain human behaviour, we lose the whole picture. Joe believes this discussion was really about the fact that they have no babies – it began with the idea that babies only smile for reasons of survival, as smiling helps the bonding between baby and parents.

Back in the present, Parry is waiting outside the flat. He pleads with Joe again, asking for *'forgiveness'*. Joe escapes inside but Parry phones him there. It is at this point that Joe starts to worry, saying: *I'm in a relationship*. The police are unhelpful because Parry has not actually committed a crime.

His anxiety makes him return to *an older dissatisfaction* about the career choices he made. Joe regards 'pure' science as the ultimate goal and feels that journalism makes him into a *parasite*. While in his twenties, he began by inventing something original, but it did not work out as planned and he lost the chance of returning to an academic science career. During that time he visited a museum, where he realized how little most people understood about dinosaurs. His insights inspired him to write a book, which was successful. He continued to make a good living from writing, but the more he did, the less chance he had of returning to research work. Now he thinks that he would like to do something meaningful in science before he turns fifty.

In the meantime, Parry has been leaving messages on the answerphone – thirty in total. The last one praises Joe for his *'brilliant idea with the curtains'*. Joe does not understand this, but we learn later that Parry reads signs into ordinary things.

Joe's article uses the ideas from a recent trend in science that believes that all or most of our behaviour comes from a genetic source. In other words, we have a sort of biological blueprint that determines how we will behave. This new approach is very different to the scientific approach after World War II and until quite recently, that emphasized how social background influenced human behaviour. This is called the 'Nature versus Nurture' debate. Clarissa's criticisms make an interesting comparison between religion and science. She complains:

> *'it's the new fundamentalism … twenty years ago you and your friends were all socialists and you blamed the environment for everyone's hard luck. Now you've got us trapped in our genes and there's a reason for everything!'*

'Fundamentalism' usually refers to strict religious beliefs, but Clarissa uses the word here to mean that science has become too dogmatic. 'Environment' here means our social surroundings and ways of organizing our societies. In fact, many scientists believe that the nature/nurture split is not so clear-cut.

Science does not exist in a vacuum; governments and businesses are all influenced by its ideas, and that affects everyone eventually.

Once again we are reminded of the gap in Clarissa and Joe's lives. For her, understanding the scientific basis of the smile (to make parents love and protect their baby) does not really explain the incredible bond that develops between parents and child. The sad thing is that Clarissa understands this love but cannot give it to a child of her own.

A lot of what Joe thinks about in this chapter might be described as 'fate'. The choices that we make (or don't make) in our twenties can affect the rest of our lives, although we are not always aware of that at the time. Now Joe is full of regret for making the 'wrong' decisions about science.
✪ Should he accept his life as it is or follow his dream?

Over to you

(Answers at end of Commentary)

? (a) How does Joe describe his feelings the day after the accident?
  (b) What does he do at the meeting with the producer and why?
  (c) What does he see out of the corner of his eye at the library?
  (d) What is Clarissa's reaction when she eventually hears about Parry?
  (e) What is one of the effects of Parry's stalking regarding Joe's career?
  (f) What do we learn in Chapter 8 about the differences between Clarissa and Joe's attitude to modern science?

? Make a Mini Mind Map of your knowledge about Parry up to this point in the novel. Have your feelings about him changed or not? Why?

Fear, obsession and a stalker. Take a break before discovering that things really can get worse!

Section 3, Chapters 9–12
Joe and Clarissa's relationship begins to break down

Chapter 9 *A wild look about him*

◆ Joe writes the chapter from Clarissa's point of view.
◆ She arrives home after a bad day at work. Joe comes across as irrational and insensitive.
◆ They have a row. He walks out in anger.

We first hear about the pressures of Clarissa's day at work. By beginning like this, Joe is trying to explain the root of their problems. His anxiety makes him miss Clarissa's signals and the repercussions of their clash make his problems much more difficult later in the novel. One 'throwaway' hint about part of her mood is included – her missing appointment diary. The clue is easy to miss, because it is just thrown in with the list of difficulties in her day. We do not understand its significance until we read Appendix I. ✪ Can you find the answer?

Not only has Clarissa experienced a stressful day, she feels physically unwell. Finally, the disturbance caused by the balloon accident is still with her, described as *a smell on the end of her fingers*.

Her first glimpse of Joe is not promising: *He has a wild look about him.* All Clarissa wants is some human contact and care, but he is too far-gone to be aware of anyone else's needs. She decides to take a bath to relax herself, but he is insensitive to this and hangs around, *like some newly discovered non-stop talking ape*. Clarissa does not understand how upset he is after the Parry incidents that day and the self-doubt that followed them. She needs time to wind down, but isn't given the opportunity to do so. Eventually Joe realizes that she is staring at him oddly and he stops talking at her.

He tells her about the phone calls and the effect that Parry is having on his work. Unfortunately, Joe has seemed so irrational beforehand that she says: *'He's not the cause of your agitation, he's a symptom.'* The conversation goes downhill from then on. He becomes defensive, and angry that she does not believe him, then she reacts badly to his anger. They get caught in petty jibes (digs) that only make the argument more painful and upsetting. When Joe leaves the apartment in a temper, Parry is hanging around outside.

Joe's regrets about the way he handled their meeting remind us of Chapter 1's reflections on fate. If he had known about her stressful day, he could have treated Clarissa with more care. If he had been less desperate to tell her about Jed Parry, if he had given her time to relax and had listened to the stories of her day… . Unfortunately, his fears about Parry make him insensitive to her needs and those crucial few moments when she arrives home have a profound effect on their relationship.

Clarissa feels unwell on her return home and recognizes that the shock of the accident may have made her vulnerable to a virus. Later, her use of the word *symptom* angers Joe because it suggests that he may be mentally unstable.

LANGUAGE, STYLE AND STRUCTURE

This chapter is the first that is not written by Joe in the first person. Instead, he uses the third person and tries to give us something of Clarissa's point of view: *… or at least, from that point as I later construed it.* The chapter is written from hindsight, in that Joe shows an awareness of how he must have seemed to Clarissa that he did not have at the time. It gives the first clear sign of the strain that Jed Parry's behaviour is placing on their relationship.

Chapter 10 *'Little secret signals'*

◆ Joe is full of self-pity and anger.

◆ Parry follows him, pleading and cursing. He believes that Joe is sending him signals.

◆ Something Parry says about the curtains triggers a faint memory in Joe.

◆ Joe returns hoping to patch things up with Clarissa.

Joe feels like a martyr, as if no one understands him, but uses the word *theatrical* as an admission that he is being a bit self-pitying. Note that Joe admits to his childish reactions in hindsight, not at the time.

Parry's disturbed behaviour angers Joe whilst comforting him – he is even more convinced of his sanity after hearing the younger man's outburst. Importantly, Parry's reference to *'signals'* triggers his memory. The hope of a clue cheers him up. He feels confident that he can convince Clarissa that he is *obviously, incontrovertibly right* and patch up their quarrel. As yet he cannot admit to his own part in the argument: *not because I had behaved badly or was wrong*. ☻ How do you think Clarissa will react to him in this mood?

LANGUAGE, STYLE AND STRUCTURE

Chapter 10 is a short break between the emotional intensity of the previous chapter and the letter from Parry in Chapter 11. Clarissa has good reasons for being sceptical about Joe's version of events, so it is important that we are reminded how extreme Parry's behaviour really is. McEwan places Joe outside, as if the fresh air and the sight of Parry are a short burst of reality to remind him of what he is up against. However, Joe's self-awareness is not what it should be. Although calmer, he still fails to understand why his behaviour has alarmed Clarissa.

Chapter 11 *'I know that you'll come to God'*

- ◆ The chapter is written as a love letter from Parry.
- ◆ He believes that Joe has left 'messages' for him on the bushes.
- ◆ He is convinced that Joe is in denial about their love, yet he is ecstatic.

'I praise God that He has sent me to you.'

The tone of the letter is a strong contrast with Parry's aggressive behaviour in the previous chapter. His illness makes him unable to accept that Joe does not return his love, so he twists the story to fit his fantasies. From his point of view, Joe immediately sensed the love between them at the site of the balloon accident, but he (Parry) was too stupid to understand it. He believes that the shock of this 'rejection' made Joe angry, so the letter is in turn ecstatic and humble. *I'll never stop saying I'm sorry. Joe, will you ever forgive me?*

 Being in love with someone can transform the way that we see life. Parry is no different. He writes movingly of the beauty around him and says: *love has given me new eyes ... I feel so alive, so alert with love.* He also believes in magical signs and is overwhelmed with happiness because he thinks that Joe has left a message in the leaves. *What a fabulous way to hear of love, through rain and leaves and skin, the pattern woven through the skein of God's sensuous creation unfolding in a scorching sense of touch.* Beautiful and sensual though the words are, they have no bearing on real life: he is imagining things.

LANGUAGE, STYLE AND STRUCTURE

Parry's ecstatic language is both like a love letter and mystical writing. This is partly because he believes himself to be in love, but his emotions are channelled through powerful religious feelings.

Ironically, considering Parry's attitude to science, he uses technological rather than spiritual metaphors. *Happiness running through me like an electrical current; the unspoken love between us as strong as steel cable.* He uses another to explain how little they know about each other's everyday life, despite the spiritual connection he believes they share. *Exploration has begun of the ocean floor, but the surface remains undisturbed.*

Chapter 12 *Losing the trick of keeping it going*

◆ The recent events bring Joe to another crisis about his failure as a scientist.

◆ He drives to visit Jean Logan, widow of the dead man.

◆ Clarissa's sceptical reaction to Parry's letter fills Joe with doubts.

◆ Joe realizes that he is visiting the widow to ease his own conscience about Logan's death.

Joe is filled with self-doubt about his career once more. He decides to drive to Oxford to visit Jean Logan, instead of brooding in his study. Notice how he mentions the possibility of Parry following him. Already he is feeling hunted. The curtain memory returns but he still cannot identify it.

He backtracks to his morning with Clarissa. Although they are no longer arguing, there are too many things that disturb Joe. Firstly, Clarissa suggests that Parry's handwriting is rather like Joe's, which suggests that maybe she wonders if Joe wrote the letters. Joe is confused. *I thought that there remained between us an unarticulated dispute, though I wasn't certain what it was.* Clarissa adds that Joe is *disturbed*, and thinks that his obsession with returning to science is related to his concern about Parry. She says to Joe: *'You're so alone in all this, even when you speak to me about it ... There's something you're not telling me.'* Joe is confused because he cannot see that the balloon accident might have changed his behaviour. In his eyes, he is speaking as truthfully as ever, so he begins to doubt Clarissa's motives. Is she looking for a way out of the relationship?

His paranoia makes him search through her study for proof of an affair, another example of Parry's effect on their relationship. Later, his guilt about doing so makes him even more self-conscious with her, adding to their difficulties. *I had crossed and re-crossed the line of my own innocence.* ❸ Why do you think that Parry's behaviour affects the couple in this way? Would being stalked affect most relationships in that way, or do Joe and Clarissa have special problems?

The next day, Joe receives a rejection letter from his science professor, which he compares to his actions in Clarissa's study: *... a parallel development, the death of an innocent dream.*

He feels as if he is *getting nowhere* and as he drives towards Oxford, he becomes confused about the prospect of *keeping a rendezvous* [an appointment] *with real death.*

It has been suggested that therapy is a modern-day substitute for religion, rather like confessing to a priest. Joe considers therapy to help with his problems – *the talking cure* – but says he has lost *faith* in it. Shortly afterwards, he uses the word *purification*, which also has religious and spiritual connotations. Indeed, his visit to Jean Logan is rather like a religious confession. He is desperate to get rid of his guilt about her husband's death.

As Joe says, *self-consciousness is the destroyer of erotic joy.* In other words, when a couple begin to distrust each other and to be over-aware of their own feelings and those of their partner, they cannot relax enough to make love. This creates even more barriers between them. The effect on Clarissa and Joe is rather like the death of innocence between Adam and Eve in the Garden of Eden.

Joe makes excuses about rummaging through Clarissa's study. He lies to himself, but realizes what he is doing. Jealousy and insecurity make him act wrongly. Joe refers to Parry's letters as *viral spore.* Later, when he is spying in Clarissa's study, he argues with himself: *what are you doing in here? Trying to stain us with your poison!* His relationship with Clarissa seems to be 'infected' by Parry's influence in their lives.

LANGUAGE, STYLE AND STRUCTURE

Some critics believe that Jed Parry is a bit like Joe's **doppelgänger** (a ghostly 'other self'). Indeed, Joe reminds himself of Clarissa's criticism that he has 'encouraged' Parry's behaviour by tactless behaviour. *He was the kind of phantom that only I could have called up, a spirit of my dislocated, incomplete character.* ✪ What do you think at this point in the novel? Do you agree with Clarissa?

Test yourself

(Answers at end of Commentary)

❓ (a) What is different about the narration of Chapter 9?

(b) Choose the words that best fit Joe's behaviour in Chapter 9:
caring; insensitive; manic; thoughtful; unreasonable; self-aware; self-centred; disturbed; loving; nurturing; selfish.

(c) Choose the words that best fit Clarissa's behaviour in Chapter 9:
relieved; tense; relaxed; exhausted; irritable; understanding; patient; sensitive; tolerant.

(d) What is the effect of Chapter 10's style after Chapter 9?

❓ Now that you have discovered more about Joe and Clarissa, make a Mini Mind Map or chart to explain how your opinions about each of them have developed.

Before encountering the widow's grief, take a break.

Section 4, Chapters 13–14
The sorrow of Jean Logan

Chapter 13 *A perfect setting for sorrow*

◆ Jean Logan believes her husband was unfaithful.
◆ She shows Joe the 'evidence' and swears to 'kill' the woman if she ever meets her.

McEwan paints a dismal, depressing scene in his description of the Logan household. Although the Logans are not poor, there is a middle-class *austerity* (severe plainness) about the house. There is nothing of beauty or style. Everything is shabby and seems *a perfect setting for sorrow.* Even the gas fire seems *poisonous.* Jean Logan's sorrow silences Joe. Like many people, he does not know how to respond to grief.

Jean is angry as well as unhappy because she believes her husband was with another woman on the day of his death. For proof, she shows Joe a bag of rotting food that she believes was their picnic. (Ironically, the bag contains two apples, rather like the apple that the serpent used to tempt Eve in the Garden of Eden.) ☉ Does Jean's desperate desire for the 'truth' remind you of any other character(s) in the novel? Why does she need to know?

The gloomy living room shows no sign of the Logan children, but Joe notices a tent in the garden. Although half-collapsed, it suggests life beyond the mother's misery and is literally outside the unwelcoming house. It also hints at the friendship that develops between the children and Joe.

In the previous chapter, Joe spoils the trust between himself and Clarissa by sneaking through her study. During this chapter, the reader is introduced to Jean, a woman who believes that her late husband was having an affair. Love has turned to mistrust. Jean's anger is so mixed up with her grief that she is unable to mourn him properly. Joe is moved by what he sees: *love, and the slow agony of its destruction.* It makes him imagine the horror of losing Clarissa and he becomes determined to solve the difficulties in his own relationship.

LANGUAGE, STYLE AND STRUCTURE

The descriptions of Jean Logan are of a woman frozen by sorrow. *She looked a long way off, out on her own in unspeakable weather, like a lone Arctic explorer.* She also seems disorientated: *for her, suffering the way she was, a social encounter like this must have been like drunk driving.*

Chapter 14 *'I know what killed him'*

◆ Jean Logan is bitter and angry.
◆ Her children discuss morality with Joe.
◆ Joe's 'curtain memory' is triggered by their game.

◆ Jean asks Joe to phone Parry, to find out if he saw Logan's mistress.
◆ She is convinced that her husband risked his life to prove himself to another woman.
◆ First mention of de Clérambault, the man who identified the 'false love syndrome'.

While Jean is trying to persuade Joe to help her find the identity of her husband's mistress, Joe's thoughts are split between a number of things. First, his guilt about Logan's death makes him agree to help Jean to find the 'truth', even though she wants him to talk to Parry. The parallels between Jed Parry and Jean are emphasized when Joe asks himself, *was my life to be entirely subordinate to other people's obsessions?* Next, the children's noisy play helps him to remember a case study. A French woman became convinced that a British king was in love with her and that he was teasing her by sending secret signals. ✪ Why is Joe so excited about this memory and who does the woman remind him of?

Despite the depressing household, Joe is inspired by the memory of the curtains. Note that he refers to this as *my own obsessions*. ✪ Do Joe's reactions remind you of his behaviour elsewhere in the novel?

[??] Jean Logan's threats about her husband's lover make her children discuss *moral relativism* with Joe. In other words, are there absolute rights and wrongs, or do these vary according to different cultures and times? Leo Logan believes that killing is always wrong, but there are many occasions when humans break this rule – war being one obvious example. ✪ Can you find other examples of moral relativism in the novel?

Tellingly, Joe's first reference to children in the chapter is about a conversation that he once had with Clarissa about their childlessness. Secondly, he remembers the pity he felt for adults and their boring lives when he was a child. Knowing this makes him self-conscious with children. He is also aware of Rachael and Leo's embarrassment about their mother's behaviour. Nonetheless, he enjoys speaking to them and they respond well to him.

As the eldest child, Rachel is most aware of her mother's unpredictable behaviour. Leo is younger but even he is provoked into an argument about killing being wrong after he hears his mother's threats. ✪ Is Jean Logan wrong to voice such feelings in the hearing of her children? Would you be able to control your feelings if you thought your partner had died because of an affair with someone else?

Joe's scientific training is seen when he tries to reason with Jean Logan. She is convinced that John Logan was having an affair, but has very little evidence. Her conviction is based on knowledge of her husband. Joe thinks to himself: *I also knew the cautionary tag from my distant laboratory days – seeing is believing ... this was a theory, a narrative that only grief, the dementia of pain, could devise.* This desire for solid evidence is ironic when contrasted with Joe's insistence to Clarissa that Jed Parry was following him. Like Jean Logan, Joe also had a 'gut feeling'. In fact, Joe is right about Parry, whereas Jean is actually mistaken about her husband, as we discover at the end of the novel.

Test yourself

(Answers at end of Commentary)

(a) How does the description of Jean Logan's household emphasize her state of mind?
(b) What does Jean Logan blame for her husband's death?
(c) How do her children react to her threat?
(d) What does Joe remember and why is it important?

We move from a widow's sorrow to the breakdown of a relationship. First, take a break.

Section 5, Chapters 15–16
Parry's threats begin and Clarissa discovers Joe's treachery

Chapter 15 *'I've got nothing to hide from you'*

- ◆ Joe returns to the scene of the accident.
- ◆ He hopes that an understanding of de Clérambault's syndrome will 'cure' his problems.
- ◆ Jed Parry is outside Joe's home again.
- ◆ Joe's scientific articles anger Parry. He makes veiled threats.
- ◆ Joe's earlier confidence leaves him.
- ◆ He finds Clarissa in his study – she confronts him about spying on her.

Returning to the scene of the balloon accident, Joe thinks about its devastating after-effects. He tries to picture Logan's lover on the day as she saw him fall. Life has changed so dramatically since that day that Joe cannot *imagine a route back into that innocence.* He hopes that de Clérambault's research will help him to understand Parry so that he can repair his relationship with Clarissa.

On his return home, Parry is waiting for him and insists on giving Joe an envelope. It contains an angry letter attacking Joe's scientific articles. Their logic challenges Parry's beliefs. *'You'll never destroy what I have. It can't be taken away'*, he argues. ✪ In hindsight, is Parry correct? Joe senses a threat. *Something had shifted in his manner … there was a hardness.* Parry's actual words puzzle Joe. *'I can get people to do things for me. Anything I want.'* Parry's changing moods make it difficult for Joe to be sure whether there is real danger in his words or not and Joe is puzzled by this *ambiguity.*

When he returns to the apartment another threat appears – the future of his relationship with Clarissa. He is shocked to find her in his study. After discovering that he had been raking through her letters, she went in there to do the same with his. It is a measure of her anger and hurt that she does not do so. As she says, *'I couldn't raise the curiosity … I don't care about your secrets.'* She is so hurt that she has run out of interest in him.

Ironically, she uses the same word as Parry to describe how she found out about Joe's spying. *'You even left the drawer open so I'd know when I came in … it's a signal.'* Of course, unlike Parry's mystic 'signals' this really is true. Joe did not mean to leave the drawer open but the physical evidence of his spying on her is certainly a 'sign' of the problems between them. And unlike Parry, Clarissa has no convenient interpretation for Joe's 'message,' she is just hurt and confused.

Joe's use of the word *innocence* to describe life before Logan's death – the 'fall' – is another reminder of the Adam and Eve story. It is as if he and Clarissa have 'fallen from grace'. Their relationship is in tatters, whereas before it was full of innocent love and trust.

He also refers to the accident scene as his *stations of the cross*, which in Christianity represent the different stages in Christ's agonizing journey to the cross where he was crucified. By using this emotive metaphor, McEwan emphasizes the suffering that Joe feels. However, it may also be a hint that Joe has a tendency to be over-dramatic and self-pitying. ✪ What do you think?

Joe uses the words *stricken* and *morbidity* to describe Parry's love for him. This makes love sound like a fatal disease rather than a blessing – and of course, he is right in this case because Parry's love springs from a mental illness and is potentially dangerous. Further into the chapter Joe repeats the connection between sickness and love, only this time he emphasizes that Parry's illness is like a *dark distorting mirror that reflected and parodied a brighter world of lovers whose reckless abandon to their cause was sane.* In other words, de Clérambault's syndrome (like many other mental illnesses) is just an extreme, out-of-control version of an ordinary human emotion. When he escapes from Parry he describes it as a *painkiller*.

LANGUAGE, STYLE AND STRUCTURE

In Chapter 15, the author uses the conventions of the thriller genre in a more subtle way. Instead of the predictable device of a criminal lying in wait at the apartment, the surprise element is that Clarissa has uncovered Joe's guilty secret. McEwan builds up the suspense when Joe returns home by giving us lots of 'clues' about Clarissa's presence, such as her work shoes in the bedroom. Joe assumes that she has gone out. His study is the last place he expects to find her and he is genuinely shocked to see her there. The suspense comes from an emotional rather than a physical threat – an attack on the couple's relationship.

Chapter 16 *Your articles add up to a long cry of loneliness*

◆ Parry's letter accuses Joe of intellectual and spiritual arrogance.
◆ He insists that: Joe will realize the error of his ways eventually; they will be together; Joe must never ignore him.

We get an idea of Jed Parry's obsession with Joe from the fact that he has paid a student £500 to photocopy all Joe's articles. Although Joe's writing goes back many years, Parry assumes that everything was written to hurt him. *I read each article as a letter sent by you into the future that was going to contain us both.*

Parry's mood is not so ecstatic now and he questions what God wants him to do. *Was I to deliver into His hands the author of these hateful pieces against him? Perhaps I was intended for something simpler and purer.* ✪ What do you think Parry means by this? Given that he thinks Joe wrote out of *contempt*, what might Parry believe Joe deserves?

Further hints of Parry's aggression can be found when he writes: *You were asleep, unaware of your own vulnerability.* On the surface he means that we are all alive because of God's protection, but it is possible to read a more threatening meaning into his words. Soon afterwards, he adds, *I worry for what your arrogance could bring down on you.*

What makes Jed Parry believable is that he is intelligent and some of his ideas make a certain amount of sense. Just as Joe finds himself drawn into the younger man's emotional mind-set, the reader half-sympathizes with Parry's ironic comments. *There's no problem with Joe Rose. His world is in place, everything fits, and all the problems are with Jed Parry.* In one way, Parry is right: Joe is not as happy with his life as we first thought. Like many of us, he is full of regret and self-doubt. Parry is mentally ill, but like many people labelled 'mad', he sometimes stumbles on the truth.

Nonetheless, Parry is highly contradictory. Not only does he speak of divine love and punishment in the same breath, we also get a sense of his backwardness when he pours scorn on the idea of a *woman novelist* inventing God. ✪ Would he have said a 'male novelist' with quite such emphasis, do you think?

Parry shows steely determination. *Your life is about to be upended. You have to tell Clarissa, you have to move all your stuff.* There is no doubt in his mind that he can make this happen. He ends with an emphatic warning: *Never deny my reality … never, never try to pretend to yourself that I do not exist.* ✪ How do you think such statements make Joe feel?

Parry declares that he believes science is a *wonderful thing,* an *extended prayer, a celebration of the glory of God's universe.* Yet he has little or no understanding of even basic science and is reluctant to accept scientific evidence if it goes against his (unproven) beliefs. ✪ What do you think? Is it possible to be religious and accept proven scientific discoveries, or are science and religion incompatible?

For Parry, there is no such problem. He says that *faith alone* is the key, not *facts, or pretend facts, or intellectual arrogance.* ✪ It might be worth looking back at the notes on the Enlightenment and Romanticism in the 'Context' section to remind yourself of why freedom of scientific discovery was so important to the foundations of modern Western society. If we rely on faith alone, what might be the result? Do you know of past and recent history about some effects of faith-led societies?

On the other hand, science does not always get it right. At least, the uses of science are not always good for humankind. Many people feel that it is out of control and fear its effects on the future.

LANGUAGE, STYLE AND STRUCTURE

Chapter 16 is in the form of a letter from Parry, which allows the reader a direct insight into the way that his mind works.

We get to hear his 'voice' without Joe's opinions on it. Letter-writing allows the writer to explore ideas in more depth than in a conversation. It is also one-sided, so Jed can preach at Joe without interruption! Disturbing though Jed's ideas are, there is also a sense of genuine passion and sincerity that is quite moving in places. The personal viewpoint allowed in a letter takes Jed's character beyond the stereotype of the madman, with the result that he becomes more believable as a character.

Finally, Jed uses a striking metaphor, comparing the universe to a recipe, with God as the divine cook: *describing how the soup is made isn't the same as knowing why it's made, or who the chef is.* ✪ What do you think about this statement? Is there any truth in it?

Test yourself

(Answers at end of Commentary)

(a) What is the name of the psychiatric condition that Joe has discovered and who does he believe is suffering from it?

(b) What has Parry read recently and how does he react to it?

(c) With what does Clarissa confront Joe?

(d) How does McEwan use the conventions of the thriller in Chapter 15?

(e) What narrative device is used in Chapter 16 and why?

Give yourself a short break. Let the ideas run through your memory before returning to the novel.

Section 6, Chapters 17–19
Matters come to a head

Clarissa ends the relationship; the police won't do anything to stop Parry; Joe is almost killed by Parry's hitmen in the restaurant.

Chapter 17 *I knew that I was on my own*

◆ The narrative returns to Joe.
◆ Joe is now receiving three or four letters a week from Parry.
◆ Clarissa doubts Joe's sanity and ends the relationship.
◆ Joe continues to hunt for Logan's mistress.
◆ He realizes he is on his own.

Jed Parry is now sending letters to Joe on a regular basis. They indicate frequent mood swings from anger to love, and 'proof' of their destiny together from his dreams and visions. Most worrying are the subtle threats, but there is not enough evidence for Joe to convince the police. Joe is frightened because the research on de Clérambault's syndrome shows that many male sufferers attempt violence.

By this time, Parry is stalking Joe on most days. However, he seems to have made a decision not to talk, which makes it difficult for Joe to obtain recorded evidence of his threats. Jed's behaviour is unpredictable. *The pattern of his love was not shaped by external influences … his was a world determined from the inside.* In other words, Jed twists everything he sees, feels or hears to his own private meaning. *Nothing could prove him wrong, nothing was needed to prove him right.* For this reason it is impossible to reason with Parry and it is this that frightens rational Joe more than anything. Joe even considers defending himself. ✪ Does this chapter make us feel less or more understanding about Jed Parry than the previous one that is written by him? Why?

Added to the constant worry that Joe feels about Parry is the breakdown of his relationship with Clarissa. Trust and open communication between them have disappeared: *To her I was manic, perversely obsessed … and the thieving invader of her private space … she was disloyal, unsupportive in this time of crisis, and irrationally suspicious.* When Clarissa finally announces that the relationship is over, Joe goes numb; he is *in a state of denial.* Despite Joe's explanations about Parry she is unconvinced. She has never seen Parry near their apartment and his handwriting is similar to Joe's. She thinks that Joe invented everything after the balloon accident sent him into shock and that he needs psychiatric help. He feels very isolated.

Whatever Joe's faults, he keeps his promises, as we discover from his attempts to help Jean Logan. One of the witnesses he speaks to, Joseph Lacey, seems willing to talk about what he noticed before the accident, but only after Joe emphasizes the torture that Jean is going through.

The slow disintegration of the couple's relationship is described with a sense of Joe's bewilderment. He feels their love slipping away but feels powerless to stop it. McEwan puns on an everyday metaphor like 'losing heart', which means 'losing hope'. *We knew we had lost heart, we had lost our heart … we didn't know how to begin talking about it.* The contrast between their uncertainty and Jed Parry's unshakeable belief that he and Joe have a relationship is ironic. Parry's other love is God, so he feels strong in his faith, however much of an illusion it really is. On the other hand, Joe cannot understand how his own relationship can fade so fast. *Didn't love generate its own reserves?*, he asks with desperate hope.

Joe imagines that Clarissa sees him as *a giant polyp of uninspired logic.* (A polyp is a growth that can occur in the body.) This makes him sound both dangerous and unattractive and is a mark of his shame and low self-esteem. In addition to such specific references, Parry's psychiatric illness is like an 'infection' that spreads doubt and fear to others, namely Joe and Clarissa. We see its damaging effects increase throughout the chapter until it finally 'kills' their love.

LANGUAGE, STYLE AND STRUCTURE

Joe describes the silence between them as *so rich as to have a visual quality, a sparkle or hard gloss, and a thickness too, like fresh paint.* These words suggest the strength and impenetrable quality of the barrier between them, as well as giving a sense that it is a new situation.

The way that the chapter is constructed also adds to the atmosphere. For example, when he and Clarissa lie in bed together, the silence between them makes Joe retreat into his memories of Parry's recent harassment. When she finally tells him it is all over, he is so stunned that his mind escapes to another recollection: *my cold-blooded thoughts hopped, frog-like, to Jean Logan.* Notice the way that he now links Clarissa and Jean together as *a category of women who believed themselves to be wronged and who expected something from me.* This is a sign of how much Joe feels trapped by recent events and how resentful he feels about them. In addition, this strand of the story adds yet another element of suspense – the truth about whether John Logan was having an affair.

Chapter 18 *'What do you want us to do? Arrest him?'*

◆ Preparations for Clarissa's birthday.
◆ Joe edits Parry's letters to emphasize their threats; Inspector Linley does not believe him.
◆ Joe is preparing a talk on whether religious faith might have a genetic basis.
◆ He remembers Clarissa's previous birthday.

Joe remains convinced that he is in the right and Clarissa is in the wrong about Jed. *She had done neither the research nor the thinking … she thought that her emotions were the appropriate guide.* Because of this, he understands why she believes he is mad, however *disastrous* this is for their relationship.

As Joe looks through Parry's letters, we begin to understand more about his fears. For example, Parry relives the satisfaction that he got from shooting rabbits as a teenager, referring to it as the *power of death that leaped from my fingers.*

The police station does not inspire Joe or the reader with optimism. Joe leads a comfortable middle-class existence, so the station's squalor is quite a shock. His interview with Inspector Linley is equally uninspiring. Ironically, Joe finds himself in a similar position to Parry. Just as Parry has no conclusive proof of his religious beliefs, Joe has no way of convincing the policeman that he is in danger. Although the police refuse to help him, at least he knows where he stands, describing the meeting as *clarifying*. We get a strong sense of Joe's determination, although we do not know what his intentions are.

Joe returns home, where he works on his latest article. It is about the possibility of a gene being responsible for religious belief. Next, he remembers Clarissa's previous birthday. The intimacy that they experienced a year ago is another reminder of his loss. Nonetheless, Joe is determined that he will *get them back to where they were*.

Joe analyses Parry's spiritual beliefs. As he points out, Parry's religion is *dreamily vague ... his belief was a self-made affair, generally aligned to the culture of personal growth and fulfilment*. In other words, none of Jed's beliefs are rooted in a recognized theological theory. Joe disagrees with all forms of religion, but he does appreciate that most important religious ideas have come about through serious debate and that a body of people is responsible for these beliefs. Unlike those involved with organized religions, Parry is unaccountable. He can invent whatever he likes, whenever he likes; therefore there is no possibility of discussion or debate. Joe's mention of *personal growth* refers to the spiritual 'self-improvement' movement, loosely based on psychotherapy, and sometimes guilty of the kind of intellectually sloppy thinking that Joe, a scientist, would hate.

Joe is also quite scornful of Parry's ignorance about Christianity. *His only concession to a source beyond himself was a couple of references to the story of Job, and even here it was not obvious that he had read the primary material.* (In other words, Parry has not studied the Bible, the basis of Christianity.) ✪ Is Joe just being intellectually arrogant, as Parry would claim, or is he right to expect some consistency in a set of religious beliefs?

The second reference to spirituality is Joe's lecture about the possibility of a genetic cause for spiritual belief. For this to be true there would have to be a connection with human survival. Joe suggests reasons such as *status* in a tribe or *single-mindedness*. Notice Joe's cynicism about religion. *Uplifted by a crazed unity, armed with horrible certainty, you descend on the neighbouring tribe, beat it and rape it senseless and come away burning with righteousness.* In other words, religious belief gives groups of human beings the justification to inflict their ideas forcibly on 'unbelievers'. ✪ Do you agree with Joe or do you think he is ignoring some good things about religion? Can you think of any examples of religious oppression, past or present?

There is only a brief mention of children in this chapter and that is of the two nameless *kids in black puffa jackets.* We learn nothing much about them, but their *slumped posture* and unexplained anger, as well as their scornful treatment by Linley, hints at the quality of their lives. Their experiences are probably very different from those of the middle-class children whom Joe would usually encounter.

There are references to the different aspects of love in a relationship. Joe describes an unusual moment with Clarissa on her previous birthday. As she began to make love to him, he pretended to be uninterested and kept reading the newspaper. Although reading and sexual activity are in two different places in the brain, Joe found to his surprise that he could be 'in two places at once'. This is typical of Joe's scientific mind, but it is also a touching memory of how close he and Clarissa were at that time.

It is not only the closeness of sex that he misses but their mental rapport. Describing a joke between them he realizes *how sharply I missed our old life together, and I wondered how we would ever return to such love and fun and easy intimacy.* The fact that these thoughts appear at the end of the chapter is another sad hint that the couple's relationship is coming to an end. Nonetheless, Joe has not given up entirely. Notice that he says *how*, not 'if' they will get back to normal.

LANGUAGE, STYLE AND STRUCTURE

Despite Joe's troubles he retains some humour. As he busies himself assembling evidence for the police, he makes a wry comment on the temporary peace this brings him. *This patient activity brought on in me a kind of organisational trance, the administrator's illusion that all the sorrow in the world can be brought to heel with touch-typing, a decent laser printer and a box of paperclips.* The attempt to cure the world's sorrow with something banal like paperclips is an amusing contrast – what is known as 'from the sublime to the ridiculous'.

His detailed descriptions of the police station and its inhabitants emphasize the despair that he observes while there. *Where the human need for order meets the human tendency to mayhem ... you find ... a great deal of general wear and tear ... stringy holes ... hot, exhausted air ... slumped posture ....*

Chapter 19 *It should have been me*

◆ Joe arrives at the restaurant booked for Clarissa's birthday dinner.
◆ She accepts gifts from Jocelyn and Joe.
◆ There is a growing sense that something is about to happen.
◆ Clarissa retells a story about Keats.
◆ Masked men shoot a diner at a nearby table. Parry prevents the second shot before escaping. Joe believes himself to be the real target.

Joe walks into the busy restaurant to find Clarissa the centre of attention. Despite their recent problems, she is welcoming and flirtatious. As she unwraps the DNA brooch given to her by her scientist godfather, Jocelyn Kale, Joe refers briefly to *the solitary diner who sat twenty feet away with his back to us.* In hindsight, we realize that the man is Jed Parry, but Joe gives us only a hint at this point in the chapter. The party discusses the history of DNA before Joe gives his present to Clarissa. It is an expensive first edition of Keats' poems and she is delighted.

The conversation turns to younger men oppressed by older men such as fathers and teachers. It begins with the DNA scientists and moves on to the relationship between Keats and his idol, the poet Wordsworth.

Joe breaks up the narrative to wish that he could have prevented the tragedy, even though it has not happened at this point in the chapter – he is writing in hindsight. This adds to the reader's confusion and anxiety. Then, as the story returns to the party, Joe sees two masked men approach the party of diners next to them. Joe assumes the men are involved in a practical joke or birthday surprise. He even describes the gun carried by one of the hitmen as a *black stick.*

'It should have been me.'

Although the incident itself is very quick, it is described as if in slow motion, like a nightmare. Ironically, it is only Jed Parry's quick reactions that save the man from a second bullet. Parry then flees from the restaurant in one direction; the hitmen disappear in another. Joe suddenly realizes that the bullet was meant for him – and that Parry organized it. The composition of the diners at the next table (a woman, an older man and middle-aged man), is almost identical to his own group with Jocelyn and Clarissa. The hitmen shot the wrong man.

✑ Jocelyn's gift to Clarissa of a brooch shaped like the DNA double helix is another reminder of the wonders of science. DNA is the key to life itself, the 'blueprint' that makes every creature individual and special. Its discovery was one of the most important scientific breakthroughs in all history.
❂ What do you think Parry's reaction would be to DNA?

As Jocelyn Kale explains, the first investigations into DNA occurred in the nineteenth century, but their importance was not understood. One influential professor later dismissed the findings as *insignificant* and became stubborn about his decision. '*It became faith with him, deep faith. What he knew, he knew....*' Because of such stubbornness amongst top scientists, DNA was not fully discovered until almost a century later. Up until now, the novel has described the limitations of religious belief, those of Parry in particular. It is no coincidence that McEwan now uses the word *faith* in a scientific context, doing so to emphasize that other belief systems can be narrow-minded, not just those of religion.

🕴 The Keats first edition that Joe gives to Clarissa is a very special, expensive gift. As you already know from the 'Context' section, Keats' work can be said to emphasize the emotional side of the human imagination. Roughly speaking, Keats' ideas on Negative Capability suggest that we can just enjoy the wonders of the unexplained without searching desperately for an explanation. It is ironic therefore that Joe's gift to Clarissa stands for a viewpoint that is opposite to his own – and that their relationship is in trouble partly because each holds a different attitude to life. The gift is also a symbol of what they once had. He bought it on the morning of the balloon accident, at a time when they were still deeply in love.

There are other parallels. The conversation about Keats being snubbed by Wordsworth is significant because it reminds us of Parry and Joe. Clarissa's story describes the passionate young Keats in a way that is like Parry. *He walked the downs in a daze of creative excitement ... he was feeling high ... Keats walked up and down in front of the great man, reciting.*

✪ Is Joe at all like Wordsworth, the *notorious grouch* who offended Keats?

Furthermore, just as Parry imagines things that are not real, the incident between Keats and Wordsworth probably did not take place. Clarissa believes that it is one of many myths about older men spurning young geniuses then living to regret their arrogance. Wordsworth was supposedly difficult and bad-tempered in his late forties but improved when he reached fifty. This sounds like a reference to Joe's recent behaviour – or at least, Joe's behaviour from Clarissa's point of view.

As in the accounts of the balloon accident, Joe's words emphasize the role of fate. *If I had stood up ... I would have seen ... I knew it later ....* The feelings are worse because he knows that the bullet was meant for him, not Colin Tapp on the next table. His guilt plagues him afterwards: *on a score of sleepless nights I've been back to plead with them to leave ... I'm from a tainted future.*

A strange chain of coincidences links Parry, Joe and Colin Tapp together. Tapp and Joe are strangers to each other, yet a simple twist of fate almost kills Tapp. As Joe remarks in the opening of Chapter 2, *so much followed from this incident, so much branching and subdivision began in those early moments, such pathways of love and hatred blazed from this starting position.*

LANGUAGE, STYLE AND STRUCTURE

Ian McEwan originally intended to use Chapter 19 as the novel's opening chapter, instead of beginning with the balloon accident. Although he changed his mind, the chapter is a key one nonetheless. By only the second sentence, Joe has established a sense of tension with his comment that entering the busy, noisy restaurant was like *walking into a storm.* In hindsight, we realize the truth of this throwaway remark – he has unknowingly walked into a dangerous situation, a *storm* of another sort.

McEwan builds up the suspense with repeated references to Joe's memories of the evening. *It was all success, clarity, chatter ... when later I remembered ... if I registered at the time ... perhaps I noticed them later ...* . The repetition increases the sense that something important is about to happen. Earlier in the chapter these remarks are vague, as if he is half-glimpsing people and occurrences out the corner of his eye, but a few pages later the comments are more emphatic. *It also became difficult to disentangle what I discovered later from what I sensed at the time ... were these details I observed later ...? ... another example of the confusion hindsight can cause memory...* .

By describing Joe's memory as vague, McEwan portrays Joe as an unreliable narrator: Yet Joe as a scientist is a trained observer, so perhaps McEwan is suggesting that everyone's memory is fallible. Question a number of people present at any accident and you would get very different versions of what occurred.

To emphasize the unexpectedness of the attempted murder, McEwan shows the confusion amongst those present. For example, Joe describes one of the hitmen as carrying a *black wand ... ready to cast his spell.* This innocent description is ironic because it makes a dangerous situation seem like a fairy story.

Test yourself

(Answers at end of Commentary)

      (a) Why doesn't Clarissa believe Joe's evidence about de Clérambault's syndrome?

      (b) What gifts does she receive in the restaurant, and how do these correspond with two of the novel's central themes?

      (c) How does McEwan create suspense in Chapter 19?

      (d) What happens to Colin Tapp and why?

Surely Clarissa and the police will believe Joe now! Find out about the aftermath of the shooting – but take a break first.

Section 7, Chapters 20–3
Joe takes matters into his own hands but, despite saving Clarissa from Parry, the couple remains separated

Chapter 20 *My isolation and vulnerability*

◆ Joe tells the police about his sighting of Parry, but they still do not believe him.
◆ He considers the impossibility of human objectivity.
◆ He phones an old friend and asks him to get a gun.

Joe finds himself in a police station for the second time that day. Before he goes for the interview, Clarissa warns him: *'don't go on about your usual stuff'*. ❷ What does she mean and why is she worried about it?

Joe's fear is emphasized by the way he watches the street, fearful of another attempt on his life. The police refuse him help and it becomes clear that Inspector Linley has warned Wallace about Joe. Wallace simply points out the disparities in Joe's statement, giving Joe pessimistic thoughts about the nature of truth and human subjectivity. He gets tired of being patronized by Wallace and decides to leave, but as he does so, the policeman shows him a packet of antidepressant tablets. Despite his fear and despair, Joe's cynical sense of humour is still present: *a maniac was trying to kill me and all the law could suggest was Prozac.*

Parry is nowhere to be seen as Joe goes home, but he feels anxious nonetheless. Clarissa is asleep, so he goes through an old address book and finds Johnny B's phone number. We learn about Johnny's history. He is an 'old hippie' cannabis dealer who was taken over by organized criminals but clung to his personal code of honour. Joe is on the verge of making a dangerous decision. *I was about to step ... into a hard-edged world of consequences.* Having decided, he phones Johnny and asks for help in buying a gun.

The differing accounts given by witnesses to the restaurant attack lead Joe to thinks that humans live in *a mist of half-shared, unreliable perception ... when it didn't suit us we couldn't agree on what was in front of us.* He believes that the effects of this subjectivity are found in divorce, war and other disputes. Joe continues by thinking that science and metaphysics were *courageous inventions,* because they tried to fight the subjectivity in human beings with *disinterested truth,* but concludes gloomily, *it couldn't save us from ourselves ... there could be no private redemption in objectivity.* Notice the use of the word *redemption* (deliverance from sin), which is ordinarily used in a religious context.

While searching through his address book, Joe remembers the *middle-class crimes* committed in the past by some of his apparently respectable friends. He uses humour when referring to the female friend, once a shoplifting hippie, now a headmistress. He jokes about her move to respectability by saying she has *no tenacity* – no staying power for crime, in other words! Joe's theory is that the middle classes commit different crimes from the poor. They do not usually stoop to theft because they are protected by *a narrow band of education and money* and also, 'good taste' holds them back. ✪ Is Joe being snobbish or ironic here, do you think?

Joe's old friend Johnny B is a drug dealer. Joe justifies Johnny's occupation by saying that he deals only in cannabis, a 'soft' drug and compares him to *the earnestly committed purveyor of fine wines, or the busy proprietor of a delicatessen.* Honest, discreet and reliable, Johnny provides a service to his customers, many of whom are rich and respectable. Joe argues that alcohol is the 'drug of choice' for the older middle classes because it is legal and sociable, even though it is potentially dangerous and can make people violent. He continues by saying that abuse comes from the faults of the person using the substance, not the substance itself. To back up this idea, he mentions a long-term heroin addict who leads a *fulfilling and useful life.* ✪ Are Joe's opinions about drug use wrong or reasonable? Would you describe him as a moral or immoral man after reading this chapter?

LANGUAGE, STYLE AND STRUCTURE

The previous two chapters have brought the novel closer to the conventional thriller. McEwan has moved away from Joe's relationship problems and has returned to 'big' issues like violence and fear of attack. The restaurant scene is like something from a gangster film, except that most of the people involved are ordinary and respectable. A stranger is almost killed and Joe knows that he may be next. He tries to do the right thing by involving the police, but they dismiss him as crazy. Even Clarissa does not believe him and he now has to consider protecting himself. ✪ Think about other novels, films or television programmes that you have seen in which the hero or heroine battles single-handedly against the odds. How typical of such characters is Joe?

Joe refers to a story about an old friend who was wrongly diagnosed with a terminal illness, as a metaphor for his own feelings: *a kind of shrinking into one's core, shrinking so deeply that everything else … appeared as though on the other side of a thick glass panel.* The reference to death emphasizes Joe's fear.

Chapter 21 *They wanted the money and they wanted absolution*

◆ Johnny B takes Joe to buy the gun.
◆ Steve, Xan and Daisy are old hippie criminals, full of 'cosmic' ideas.
◆ The three housemates are reluctant to sell the gun.
◆ Steve and Xan fight over Joe's money.
◆ Johnny and Joe escape.
◆ On the way home, Joe gets a phone call: Parry is holding Clarissa captive.

Joe is in unknown territory. He is unfamiliar with the world inhabited by people who sell guns. Johnny's three acquaintances live in a run-down house with rusting motorbikes outside. The dog chain attached to the garage wall emphasizes the seedy, slightly sinister air. Even non-judgmental Johnny is forced to warn Joe, *'Don't make fun of these people. They haven't had your advantages, and they're, uh, not too stable.'* Unfortunately Joe manages to get off on the wrong foot immediately by angering Steve. The more we read about the house and its inhabitants, the more we realize that Johnny is right. Foolish and uneducated they may be, but Xan and Steve are unpredictable and violent. Joe's nervousness makes him vulnerable. He almost ruins the deal by laughing hysterically at Steve's moustache, and it is only Johnny's quick thinking that saves the situation.

The three hippies are failures and financial insecurity has made them tense and irritable. Only the woman, Daisy, makes any attempt to be civil. It is clear that they have been involved in some serious crime in the past because they bought the gun for 'protection', but they are keen to stress that they *'don't approve'* of guns. Joe's terse explanation about Parry gives them a convenient let-out: *'So it is self-defence,' Xan said with hope in his voice.* Despite their New Age beliefs, Steve and Xan grab greedily at the money then get into a dangerous fight. Daisy only makes a slight protest before walking out of the room. Joe senses that this sort of conflict happens all the time. The fight is compared to sex, such is the intensity between the men.

Joe and Johnny try to save Steve, but have to leave for their own protection. Johnny warns that they cannot afford to be associated with the household if *'something happens'.* ✪ What exactly is Johnny worried about?

Despite the recent danger, there is something comical in the way that Johnny says, *'I've been there at other times, and we've had these really interesting discussions.'* There is a skilful contrast between the ludicrousness of his remark and what happens next. McEwan takes us from violence in the house to ironic laughter in the safety of the car – before dropping the final bombshell about Parry and Clarissa.

'Someone wants to kill me.'

[?] Joe uses the religious term *absolution* (release from sin) to point out the double standards of the three hippies. They are so desperate for money that they compromise their beliefs and sell the gun. *These coke dealers ... and their dim beliefs were making a stab at being moral and they wanted me to help them out.* We have already learned that they made their money from selling cocaine, then went legal by going into property dealing. When the housing market went down, they fell on hard times but seem to believe that they are 'better' than other criminals because they read books.

The three hippies bear a resemblance to Jed Parry in their use of muddled New Age ideas without any proof or understanding. *Xan gave his judgements the ring of fundamental truth by adorning them with basically. 'Basically,' he said ...'your allergy is a form of imbalance.'* Joe's rather scornful amusement is obvious. *It was a while since I had heard this device, the percentages snatched from the air, the unprovenanced research, the measurements of the immeasurable. It had a peculiarly boyish ring.* Daisy, the middle-aged 'earth mother', also adds her analysis. *'You are unhappy ... I can see a lot of dirty yellow in your aura.'* (It does not take special powers to guess at someone's state of mind if they are buying a gun!) Daisy is very 'touchy feely', and we can almost sense Joe's relief when he thinks, *if the table had been narrower she might have reached for my hand.*

The discussion about allergies and illness in the modern world is typically ill informed. Steve is rude about Johnny's belief that the Industrial Revolution was the start of serious pollution and suggests that it is the *'state of mind'* created by industrialization that made us vulnerable to allergies. Johnny's statement at least shows recognition of environmental causes, but Steve has no proof. It is true that the Industrial Revolution changed people's lives dramatically, often destructively. However the hippies romanticize life before the Industrial Revolution, with little understanding of the whole picture.

LANGUAGE, STYLE AND STRUCTURE

Despite the dangers facing Joe and Johnny, Chapter 21 is very amusing in places. Firstly, Joe has made a careful decision to buy a gun, yet knows nothing about weapons. Then he almost ruins the deal by antagonizing Steve. As if this were not bad enough, Joe almost explodes into hysterical laughter as he looks at Steve's comical moustache. After these mistakes, Joe takes on the role of lone hero. He is desperate by now and sick of playing games.

Joe eventually stands up to the aggression of Xan and Steve. *I made a show of looking at my watch and said, 'I'll tell you in four words and nothing more. Someone wants to kill me.'* In fact, the second sentence is five words and Joe amusingly mocks his own 'tough guy' act by mentioning that everyone is counting! Joe's boldness works for a while, but the situation turns both farcical and dangerous. Steve and Xan fight over the money, so Joe and Johnny make a quick getaway with the gun. ✪ Do you think Joe is a realistic hero?

The narrative returns to serious thriller mode when Joe receives a phone call. Jed Parry is holding Clarissa prisoner in the apartment, and the chapter ends, appropriately, on a cliffhanger. It is as if McEwan wants to shock the reader. He reminds us that despite the humour of the previous scene, it is not a game; Clarissa is in real danger.

Chapter 22 *Getting things right in the worst possible way*

- ◆ Joe tries out the gun in the forest.
- ◆ After checking the building he arrives in the flat.
- ◆ Jed begins to harm himself with a knife. Joe shoots him.
- ◆ Joe is arrested.
- ◆ The situation between Joe and Clarissa remains bad.

The atmosphere in Chapter 22 is tense and edgy. We have no idea how it might turn out, although we can guess that Joe survives because the novel is written from hindsight. Despite Joe's fear, he has the foresight to try out the gun first. Most people in Europe are unfamiliar with guns. Joe is no different. He expects the gun to give off some special aura, *the mystique of deadly potential*. What he discovers is its frightening ordinariness. A gun is just a piece of metal until it is loaded and pointed at another human being. Ironically, it is the old hippie Johnny who comes to the rescue and teaches him how to use it. Joe then drives down the motorway at breakneck speed, like a true thriller hero.

Another realistic touch is the effect that fear has on Joe's bowels! Most people react like this in situations of real danger, but we do not usually learn about this in films or books – partly because of the taboo about bodily functions, partly because it might take away some glamour from the hero.
❂ Do you think this detail makes Joe seem less or more brave?

After he enters the flat Joe finds Clarissa terrified but brave. She has enough strength to warn him about Parry's state of mind. She even takes the risky step of trying to reason with the distressed younger man. *'I'm sure Joe didn't mean you any harm.'* Joe understands Parry's reaction better than Clarissa because he knows him. *We were catching a glimpse of the core of his condition; he had to block out the facts that didn't fit.* When Parry looks as if he will stab himself, Joe shoots him.
❂ Is he right to do so? What would you have done? Given Parry's unpredictable behaviour, what else might Joe be frightened of?

The chapter ends on a note of depressing anticlimax. Instead of Joe being hailed as a hero and the couple being reunited, Clarissa is upset about his use of the gun and the police arrest him for possession of an illegal firearm. He has to spend the night in a cell before being let out on bail. He is in shock. *No caresses then that night, none of the kitchen table talk and bed that had held us together in the evening after John Logan's death.* His sense of loneliness remains. Although the police do not prosecute him, he is more worried about his relationship, fearing that he and Clarissa will never be reunited.

Joe's usual comfort in science has been driven away by shock. A remark from Johnny about the behaviour of some people he knew makes Joe think, *at another time I might have been drawn to elaborate the evolutionary perspective ... but now I felt sick.* While squatting in the forest, he looks at the earth and thinks about biology. *What I thought might calm me was the reminder that we were still part of this natural dependency ... but ... I could not believe in the primary existence of these grand cycles.* No amount of perspective will take away the reality that Clarissa is in danger from a madman.

Joe's dark thoughts bring him to the following pessimistic conclusion about humanity. *We were no longer in the great chain. It was our own complexity that had expelled us from the Garden. We were in a mess of our own unmaking.* In other words, Joe believes that we have lost our way in the natural rhythms of life, that we have become too complex to exist harmoniously with nature. Ironically, Parry would probably agree with Joe here! ❂ Which *Garden* is Joe referring to, and why?

Joe takes a huge risk in rescuing Clarissa. In a conventional thriller, they would fall into each other's arms and be reunited. Instead, she is shocked and disgusted by his use of the gun. *I thought we would never get past this moment. Lately my worst suspicions had tended to be confirmed. I was getting things right in the worst possible way.* McEwan seems to be suggesting that life is never simple and people's reactions are more complex than most thrillers reveal. Perhaps we like neat, predictable happy endings precisely because real life is so messy and inconclusive ❂ Do you like this ending to the chapter or would you have preferred a happy one? Why?

LANGUAGE, STYLE AND STRUCTURE

Joe is not a stereotypical hero. He is a middle-class man with a conventional life who is drawn into danger not of his own making. Despite his fear, he is determined to rescue Clarissa. Once again, McEwan reverts to the thriller genre by making Joe get on the roof to check out the situation. In a conventional thriller, Joe might fire at Parry through the skylight, but McEwan makes the situation more realistic. Joe does not know enough about shooting to take such a risk – he might hurt Clarissa by mistake. Instead he goes to meet Parry in the apartment. He is clumsy and unconfident with the gun, not a slick gunman from an action film. ❂ Does Joe's inexperience make him less or more of a hero?

Chapter 23 *You went your own way, you denied him everything*

◆ Letter from Clarissa to Joe – her perspective on events.
◆ She apologizes for not believing him about Parry.
◆ She accuses Joe of not confiding in her and believes that Joe forced Parry into a confrontation.
◆ She wants a trial separation.

We learn that Clarissa and Joe had a serious argument after his release from the police station. Joe felt betrayed by her lack of support over Jed. Clarissa admits that she was in the wrong but believes that Joe could have prevented *the frightening outcome* by acting differently towards Parry. We also learn just how strange Joe's behaviour must have seemed to her. *I watched you go deeper into yourself and further and further away from me. You were manic, and driven, and very lonely.* As she notes, Joe acted oddly even before he knew anything about Parry's obsession.

Clarissa believes that Joe was so full of guilt and worry about the possibility that it was him who let go of the balloon rope, that he transferred these feelings onto Parry. *Isn't it possible that Parry presented you with an escape from your guilt?* ❍ Do you think that there is any truth in this? She thinks that asking Parry in to talk with them both might have calmed the situation and that everything that Joe did just made it worse. She is unconvinced about de Clérambault's syndrome so does not understand that sufferers often turn violent. ❍ knowing what you know in hindsight, do you think that Joe could have prevented the final crisis, or is Clarissa naïve?

LANGUAGE, STYLE AND STRUCTURE

Once again, we hear Clarissa's side of things, but this time directly, in the form of a letter. Many early novels were written entirely in this form, known as the epistolary novel. (An 'epistle' is an old word for a letter.) Letters give a sense of immediacy to a narrative and Clarissa's is particularly effective because it is as if we experience the shock of her disturbing message at the same time as Joe.

References to letters occur throughout *Enduring Love* as well as in this chapter. Clarissa is interested in finding lost letters from Keats, and Jed writes passionate letters to Joe. It is typical of a modern novel that McEwan uses a variety of narrators.

Test yourself

(Answers at end of Commentary)

(a) Who does Joe contact after leaving the police station and why?
(b) Who phones Joe with what news?
(c) What is the outcome?
(d) What is Clarissa's reaction to the recent events?

Poor Joe has escaped death only to be separated from his beloved. Will things ever get back to normal? Before you read on, take a well-deserved break.

Section 8, Chapter 24 to Appendix II

Loose ends are tied up. The mystery of John Logan's 'lover' is solved for Jean Logan and there is fresh hope for Joe and Clarissa. We learn more about Parry's illness and the future happiness of the couple.

Chapter 24 *Mutual forgiveness*

◆ Joe and Clarissa drive to Oxford.
◆ His feelings of betrayal remain.
◆ Jean Logan and her children accompany the couple on a picnic.
◆ Professor Reid and Bonnie Deedes arrive. The mystery of Logan's 'lover' is solved, but Jean is left feeling guilty.
◆ The Logan children ask Joe about the river.

Joe reveals that he has recently visited Joseph Lacey, although we do not yet know the outcome. (The two men had a telephone conversation in Chapter 17.) Clarissa and Joe travel to Oxford. They feel awkward together, but manage to pass the journey without another argument.

Ironically, we learn that Clarissa has been searching for an unsent love letter from Keats to Fanny Brawne, while Joe's work has been concerned with various scientific projects. Once again we see the differences between the couple being emphasized by the work each one does. Clarissa is trying to find a love letter that was never sent – an attempt to understand Keats' emotional life – whereas part of Joe's research concerns the exploration of another planet. Typically, Clarissa is not impressed with the Mars project and interprets it from a human rather than scientific viewpoint. *'What's the point? It's beautiful here and we're still unhappy.'* This is an ambiguous remark: it is unclear whether she is referring to humanity in general, or the two of them. Whatever the interpretation, Joe dreads more personal talk. He remembers their terrible argument after the kidnapping, describing it as *an orgy of mutual accusation.* Joe feels angry and betrayed. Once he might have accepted Clarissa's interpretation of the Parry crisis, but now he believes her memory and *clammy emotional logic* to be at fault, not his. They have reached a stalemate.

Joe thinks that the Logan's house represents a *boring and unproductive* yet safe life. However, this idea is contradicted by the symbolic (and comical) wildness of young Leo's appearance. He opens the front door naked, covered in body paint to look like a wolf. More seriously the sight of Jean, twisted by bitterness and grief, shatters any ideals about domestic harmony. Clarissa breaks the ice by teasing Rachael and playing with her.

The children provide a safe distraction for Clarissa and Joe. Leo and Rachael behave like typical brother and sister, acting in a competitive and jealous way over their new adult friends. Yet the siblings are also affectionate, holding hands and taking care of each other, a strong contrast with their solitary and bitter mother – and the estranged Clarissa and Joe.

Jean Logan meets Professor James Reid and his young lover, Bonnie Deedes. Reid explains that it was Bonnie's scarf that was found in John Logan's car. In other words, John was a faithful husband and it was only the lovers' fear of publicity about their affair that stopped them coming forward earlier. Lacey promised to keep their secret unless it was absolutely necessary. Once Joe told him about Jean Logan's unhappiness, Lacey contacted them.

Bonnie makes no effort to apologize or explain to Jean. Joe thinks that she is *either dim ... or contemptuous of us all.* ✪ What do you think? Is there another explanation for her silence or is Joe judgmental? Instead, Reid does all the talking. He seems genuinely sorry for causing Jean such distress. Now Jean has to live with her own guilt after learning that she was wrong about her husband. McEwan may want the reader to wonder if that is better than the hate and anger she felt previously. ✪ What do you think? Ironically, the conversation between Reid and Jean affects Joe and Clarissa, who catch each other's eye. *It was as if we were pitching in our own requests for mutual forgiveness, or at least tolerance.*

At the end of the chapter it is the children who offer the greatest hope for the future. Even though they argue, McEwan seems to be suggesting that the bonds between people who love each other can be strong enough to survive misunderstandings. Similarly, the conversation about the river may be a reminder to Joe that life is a complex, wonderful business. Perhaps Joe and Clarissa are a bit like those *'two atoms of hydrogen ... bound together by a mysterious powerful force'.* Certainly, the way that Rachael includes her brother in the final sentence hints at reconciliation between Clarissa and Joe. Joe uses the word *autopsy* to describe the argument he has with Clarissa. Its use suggests that they took each other apart emotionally in a particular unpleasant way.

Clarissa loves children, as her first meeting with Rachael confirms. Confident and playful, she makes friends with the little girl immediately. Rachael also likes Joe and continues with their conversation from the first meeting. According to her mother, she is looking for a father figure since the death of John Logan. Most importantly, the children set an example of love and support as opposed to the emotionally fragile adults.

They quarrel and get jealous over Joe, but finally unite in friendship. *'So now,'* Rachael said. *'Tell Leo as well.'*

 The word *forgiveness* is used repeatedly during the last pages of the chapter, firstly by Professor Reid, then by Jean and finally by Joe. In a religious context it means forgiveness by God for our sins. For Jean, there is no such relief because she is not religious. *'Who is going to forgive me? The only person who can is dead.'* For Joe and Clarissa it means letting go of their anger so that they can love again. Once again, McEwan uses a religious term to suggest the intensity of human feelings.

LANGUAGE, STYLE AND STRUCTURE

The preparations for a picnic echo the beginning of Chapter 1. The memory of the precious moments before the balloon accident is a bitter one for Joe now he is separated from Clarissa. The narrative continues with the solving of Jean's mystery, allowing her to make a fresh start. Clarissa and Joe's eye contact as they observe Jean's distress hints at an important breakthrough for the couple – perhaps they are close to realizing that life is too short to spend in bitterness and regret. Finally, the children of the dead man act as a reminder of the power of love and forgiveness as well as of a more hopeful future.

Appendix I

◆ It is written in the style of a scientific article about de Clérambault's syndrome.
◆ It uses Jed Parry's story as a case history to illustrate the effects of the disease. The appendix clears up the last of the story's loose ends concerning Parry, Joe and Clarissa.

The article achieves a number of goals. It lets us know what happened to Joe and Clarissa's relationship in amongst a detailed psychiatric explanation of Parry's behaviour. It also solves the mystery of how he planned the restaurant shooting. He stole Clarissa's diary from her workplace and found out about her birthday party. (Find the hint in the first paragraph of Chapter 9.) This detail proves Joe's claims about Parry and the hitmen. Finally, we discover that Joe and Clarissa are reunited and later adopt a child, something that was missing from their relationship.

Parry's illness is explained. *In the pure form of the condition onset was precise and sudden, even explosive.* The balloon accident created an emotional trigger that pushed him into madness. Secondly, de Clérambault sufferers are convinced that the person they love began the affair, and cannot be persuaded that these feelings come from a mental illness. This explains Parry's anger towards Joe. He genuinely believed that Joe set the whole thing up.

The appendix is convincing because it gives background information about de Clérambault's syndrome then follows it by using Parry's obsession for Joe as a case history. It explains how a sufferer's life is changed by the illness – and how a sufferer can affect the life of the one with whom they fall in love. We also learn more about Jed's background and the childhood isolation that may have made him prone to such an illness.

In addition, we learn about the psychiatric tests that make Parry seem relatively normal. Although unstable, he expresses his belief in Joe's love in an *articulate and coherent* way.

❍ What do you now think of Joe and Clarissa's opinions about Parry? Does this part of the novel prove that Joe was correct to behave as he did, or could he have handled Parry better, as Clarissa suggested? Before making a decision, look closely at what the appendix says about the attempts to cure Parry. You will find the details in the final paragraph of the *Case History* section. You may also want to re-read Appendix II.

In conclusion, McEwan seems to suggest that the line between 'normal' behaviour and madness is difficult to pin down. Even today, mental illness is often portrayed as something 'weird' and far removed from ordinary life. The novel challenges such an idea by showing how difficult situations can affect people. Think back to Joe's strange behaviour after the accident and of Jean Logan's obsessive hatred and misery. Perhaps mental illness is just an exaggerated form of strong human emotions such as love, grief or shock.

The article makes a link between pathological forms of love (love distorted by illness) and religion. Religions are often anti-sex; some psychologists believe that religious love becomes a replacement for forbidden sexual feelings – like Parry's love for Joe. ✪ What do you think? Is there some truth in the idea?

The conclusion of the appendix is an ironic reminder of the pun in the novel's title, *Enduring Love*. It states that de Clérambault's syndrome is *a most lasting form of love, often terminated only by the death of the patient.* Jed Parry's feelings for Joe are 'enduring' or lasting. Many people dream of lasting love, but Joe has no choice. He has to 'endure', or put up with, Parry's love until it almost kills him and Clarissa.

More disturbingly, the article concludes by questioning the 'normality' of love. *'The pathological extensions of love not only touch upon but overlap with normal experience, and it is not always easy to accept that one of our most valued experiences may merge into psychopathology.'* In other words, even so-called 'normal' love has an element of madness in it, which is why it can be difficult to diagnose de Clérambault's syndrome. Most cultures regard love as life-changing and important. It is therefore uncomfortable to think that love can be close to mental illness! ✪ Have you ever known of an intense love that was close to obsession or made someone act strangely?

LANGUAGE, STYLE AND STRUCTURE

After the personal narrative in Chapters 1–24, the formal style of Appendix I is a big contrast. McEwan may have used this style because it suggests scientific objectivity – the 'truth', not a personal viewpoint like the rest of the novel. Very importantly, it helps to justify Joe's opinions about Parry. ✪ Did its style make you want to believe in it? Is McEwan trying to make a point about the different ways that readers respond to texts?

McEwan also adds a bibliography (list of sources) at the end. ✪ Why has he bothered to do this?

Appendix II

◆ A letter from Parry to Joe.
◆ He declares that his love will never die.

McEwan finishes the novel with a brief but dramatic letter
from Parry. The letter is ecstatic and it is clear that he is still
deeply in love with Joe. *This happiness is almost an
embarrassment to me … I ought to be going under. Instead I
feel more purpose than I've ever known in my life … I live for
you. I love you.* The extent of Parry's delusion is startling.
Despite being imprisoned in the psychiatric hospital for three
years, he seems more in love with Joe than ever. The second
appendix is ambiguous in that Parry is given the last word in
the novel – even though he does not seem to realize that all
his letters are confiscated. In the absence of a written response
from Joe he reads signs into what he sees around him: *you
telling me that what I'm doing is right! … thank you for
recognising what I am doing for our love. Send me a new
message soon … .* This final proof of Parry's 'enduring love' is
chilling because we realize that he is incurable and therefore a
threat to Joe unless he is locked up.

Once again, Parry's love reveals religious overtones.
Remember that although he loves Joe, he does not see it
in sexual terms. Instead, he seems to see the 'relationship' as a
spiritual joining with God: *…the resplendence of God's glory
and love. Our love! … When you are His, you also become
mine.*

Parry mentions the *shuffling, muttering, dribbling idiots*
who are the other psychiatric patients. Such images of
mental illness are quite common. What is less well known is
that many mentally ill people can in many ways, or at certain
times, be 'normal'. Parry is a good example of this, being
articulate, intelligent and seemingly normal, yet capable of
extremely dangerous behaviour. Once again, McEwan shows
us that the boundaries between normal and abnormal
behaviour are often difficult to pin down.

Test yourself

(Answers at end of Commentary)

? (a) What link is there between Chapters 1 and 24?

(b) What is the answer to the John Logan mystery and who reveals it?

(c) What do the children ask Joe about? Why is it so significant to the outcome of the novel?

(d) What is the difference in style between the novel and Appendix I? Why has McEwan written it like this?

(e) Who writes Appendix II? Why does this character have the last word – and why is it so ironic?

? Make a Mind Map showing the position of the following characters at the beginning of the novel and how they end up: Joe, Clarissa, Parry and Jean Logan.

? Imagine that Jed Parry manages to sell his story to the newspapers. Write his version of events.

? Write an entry for Jean Logan's journal since she has heard the truth about her husband from Bonnie Deedes and Professor Reid. Include her regrets and also, plans for the future of herself and the children.

? Make a Mind Map or timeline of the main events in the novel in the correct order. **Hint:** you may find the Section headings useful, but add more detail.

Phew – you're at the end of the Commentary. Now take a well-earned break.

Answers to Commentary tests

SECTION 1, CHAPTERS 1–3

(a) tense and dramatic, fast-paced; (b) the expulsion of Adam and Eve from the Garden of Eden; (c) human selfishness or survival instinct; (d) Logan's death left his two children orphaned; (e) Jed Parry. Joe tells Clarissa it was a wrong number, making it difficult to convince her about Parry's madness later.

Words applying to Parry: religious, eccentric, obsessive, forceful, lonely, insensitive.

SECTION 2, CHAPTERS 4–8

(a) unease; (b) Joe rants about the accident because he is in shock and upset; (c) a flash of red and white trainers that he guesses are Parry's; (d) amused – she jokes about Joe's *'secret gay love affair with a Jesus freak!'* ; (e) the worry stirs up old insecurities about his failure as a scientist; (f) Clarissa believes that science reduces things to their parts but sometimes misses the overall point; Joe thinks that understanding things doesn't mean that they lose their wonder.

SECTION 3, CHAPTERS 9–12

(a) it is written by Joe but in the third person and from Clarissa's viewpoint; (b) insensitive; manic; unreasonable; self-centred; disturbed; selfish; (c) tense; exhausted; irritable; (d) it reminds us that Parry is aggressive and unpredictable – it isn't all in Joe's imagination.

SECTION 4, CHAPTERS 13–14

(a) it is cold and bleak; (b) she believes that he was trying to impress a lover with his bravery. He was not a risk-taker and there was picnic food for two in his abandoned car; (c) Leo argues that killing is wrong, Rachael is protective and anxious; (d) he remembers a case about a woman who believed the King was leaving secret messages via the curtains. Joe wonders if Parry may be suffering from the same condition.

SECTION 5, CHAPTERS 15–16

1. (a) de Clérambault's syndrome; (b) all Joe's scientific articles. He is angry; (c) spying on her; (d) by building up the tension towards the end of the chapter, the reader thinks there may be an intruder in the flat; (e) epistolary – a letter from Parry to Joe. It gives us a direct insight into Parry's point of view.

SECTION 6, CHAPTERS 17–19

(a) she believes he is disturbed and is using the evidence to justify his obsession with Parry; (b) the gifts represent two opposing themes – the DNA brooch symbolizes progress via the wonders of science; the first edition of Keats' poems suggests a Romantic or spiritual approach to life; (c) by giving detail about apparently unconnected events and by writing from hindsight; (d) he is mistaken for Joe by the hitmen and shot.

SECTION 7, CHAPTERS 20–23

(a) Johnny B, to buy a gun for protection – he believes that Parry will make another attempt on his life; (b) Parry phones and makes Clarissa explain that he is holding her prisoner; (c) he shoots Parry in the leg; (d) she is horrified by the shooting and blames Joe for mishandling Parry.

SECTION 8, CHAPTER 24 TO APPENDIX II

(a) each features a picnic and a reunion; (b) Bonnie Deedes and her lover Professor James Reid reveal that they were given a lift by John Logan, but fled the scene of the accident to avoid publicity; (c) about the river. It suggests the passage of time and hints at love and unity; (d) Appendix I is written like a 'true' scientific article from a respectable journal. It validates Joe's viewpoint because it seems like an objective piece of writing; (e) Parry gets the last word to remind us of his 'enduring' love and how dangerous he will always remain to Joe. It is ironic because Joe will never receive the letter.

What is the point of criticism?

Readers bring their own **cultural position** to the texts they read – assumptions about what is 'important' or 'normal' – whether they realize it or not. Critical theory shows so-called 'common sense' ideas to be a product of historical and social change. In other words, common sense is just part of a theory – **ideology** – that has come to seem so 'normal' that we don't even regard it as a theory any more!

Meaning changes over time

Remember that your values and opinions also come from your own experiences and those of the people close to you, not just the dominant ideas in society. For example, most 'typical' sixteenth-century English people might have watched a play like Shakespeare's *The Taming of the Shrew* and laughed at its portrayal of the angry Kate and her husband's attempts to 'tame' her. Nonetheless, not everyone then would have agreed, because influential political and religious groups were arguing about the role of women, amongst other things. Today, most people might enjoy the play but feel uncomfortable about the scenes in which Kate surrenders to her husband's authority.

Differences are interesting, not 'wrong'

In the past, good works of literature were said to be 'universal' – in other words, there was something in them that would appeal to our 'common humanity'. Most modern critics disagree because such a viewpoint ignores important issues of class, race, culture and gender. That doesn't mean we can't enjoy texts from different times and cultures. It simply recognizes that each of us will interpret them in different ways, according to our background – and judge them with different sets of values. Examining these differences adds an exciting dimension to our understanding of what we read and watch.

Twentieth-century criticism

There are different groups or 'schools' of literary criticism. Many have certain elements in common. If you study English after A/S and A2 Level, it is likely that you will study these in greater detail. Even if you don't agree with them, such ideas are useful to start a debate. What follows below is an introduction to some of the most influential types of literary criticism and an attempt to relate their theories to *Enduring Love*.

Marxist criticism

CLASS AWARENESS AND CLASS STRUGGLE

Marxist criticism is one well-known approach that analyses literature from the perspective of social class and class struggle, often including the role of women and that of different cultures and races. It also looks at the way texts present or avoid social realities. One striking example of this is that many of the respectable families in Jane Austen's novels would have got their wealth through the slave trade, but this is only hinted at occasionally. Such writers were making a big statement about their own attitudes and those of their society, whether this was conscious or accidental!

JOE AND CLARISSA'S LIFE TOGETHER

To give an example from *Enduring Love*, life for many people in a large city like London is very different from that experienced by Joe and Clarissa, despite what you might think from watching television. It is a city with its share of sub-standard housing, badly paid jobs and high crime rates like anywhere else. Joe and Clarissa lead a relatively charmed life. They earn a lot of money, live in an expensive part of the city and can afford to eat in fashionable restaurants.

Joe is self-employed, so does not have to deal with bosses and their demands in the way that most workers do. In contrast, Clarissa is based in a workplace and there is some hint that outside forces affect her working and personal life – her bad mood in Chapter 9 is partly because of work-related pressures. The lack of further references to these problems suggests that they will not affect her job security or satisfaction too deeply – either that, or Joe has chosen to leave out this information.

Joe is especially cut off from the lives of ordinary people. Despite living in a city with huge traffic problems, he can afford to avoid public transport and frequently travels by taxi. Furthermore, his response to the house of the three hippies and their lack of formal education suggests that he does not usually mix with people outside his own social class. There is one brief mention of the couple's cleaner, who otherwise remains invisible, yet she makes it possible for the couple to live their life as they do. To be fair, it is impossible for an author to include everyone, but the couple has so little contact with others outside their social group that this small detail reminds us that class divisions continue, even today.

Think about Joe's life as portrayed in the novel – did it make sense to you or is it light-years from the way you live? Would you feel uncomfortable being surrounded by well-off, confident academics talking about Keats and DNA, or would such a world be familiar to you because of your parents or their friends?

✪ Why does Steve react so badly to Joe's 'actually' in Chapter 21? Has anyone's accent ever made you feel out of place or stupid? Have you ever adapted your own accent to fit in with your company? Why? Do you think McEwan is making assumptions about his readership? And does it matter – do these issues get in the way of your reading or can you still enjoy the novel? After all, one of the good things about reading is the insight it gives us into other people's lives.

Feminism

Feminism was an important political movement that changed attitudes to gender roles from the 1960s onwards. Many of the changes that have taken place in women's lives – and men's – are quite recent. For example, equal pay and maternity leave are principles that we tend to take for granted in Western society, but in fact they have come about only recently.

Feminist criticism looks at the portrayal of women and men in texts. For example, Clarissa comes across as an equal in the relationship. She has her own career, co-owns the apartment with Joe, and has her own group of colleagues and friends. She is also sexually confident with Joe, frequently taking the initiative. Her life would have been unthinkable a few generations ago except for wealthy women. Yet even today, working women with children experience greater difficulties than their male counterparts.

Joe respects Clarissa; in fact he seems quite in awe of her at times. He is full of admiration for her talents, recognizing her as an intellectual equal, whilst disagreeing with her on some issues. Yet Clarissa is angry that Joe excludes her from the problem with Jed Parry – Joe's version of protecting the 'little woman', perhaps?

Anti-racism

Some critics take the view that what is omitted from a text can be important, as well as what is included. It might therefore be significant that although Joe and Clarissa live in London, a hugely multicultural city, we get little sense of them mixing with people of other nationalities or races. This is not to say that they or McEwan are racist; it may just be that they move in largely white circles, which itself says something about the relative lack of non-whites in well-paid jobs. Once again, this does not make the novel 'bad' but it gives us implicit messages about the society in which it is set. Does the lack of black characters make this novel incomplete, or can we just appreciate the story for what it is – an account of two people caught up in a terrible situation? ◐ What do you think?

What the critics said

It is usually easy to find critical articles and studies of older or longer-established texts. Modern works like *Enduring Love* take a while to gather academic analysis, but two examples from critics are given below.

Sven Birkerts praises the novel but makes the following points:

'Interesting and credible though Joe and Clarissa are, there is some way in which they don't seem thoroughly known, as if McEwan didn't trust that he had permission to imagine them all the way into existence.' ('Grand Delusion' from *The New York Times on the Web*, 25 January 1998, www.nytimes.com/books)

Cressida Connolly describes it as 'brilliant' and adds that it is 'a worthwhile attempt to view the irrational through the lens of the rational'. She does, however, believe that the novel is 'weighed down by a surfeit of scientific information' and suggests that 'novelists should tell us stories, not recite particle physics.' (*Over-Fished Waters* from *Literary Review*, www.users.dircon.co.uk)

You as the critic

Criticism is a useful and necessary part of understanding texts at A/S and A2 Level, and beyond, but it is not a substitute for your own close reading and work on a text. Knowing the text thoroughly is the best way to help form your own opinions and it will allow you to respond intelligently to the opinions of others. Perhaps you could use the two statements by Birkerts and Connolly as a starting point for discussion. A debate with one or more of your classmates would be a useful way to revise the novel.

HOW TO GET AN 'A' IN ENGLISH LITERATURE

In all your study, in coursework and in exams, learn how to explain the following where appropriate to the question:

- **Characterization** – the characters and how we know about them (e.g. speech, actions, author description), their relationships and how they develop.
- **Plot and structure** – the story and how it is organized into parts or episodes.
- **Setting and atmosphere** – the changing physical scene and how it reflects the story (e.g. a sunny day reflecting happiness, or a sunny day acting as a strong contrast to a character's misery).
- **Style and language** – the author's choice of words, and literary devices such as imagery and how these reflect the **mood**.
- **Viewpoint** – how the story is told (e.g. through an imaginary narrator and character like Joe Rose, or through an omniscient narrator who has no part in the story, like the authors of the article in Appendix I of *Enduring Love*).
- **Social and historical context** – the author's influences.
- **Critical approaches** – different ways in which the text has been, or could be, interpreted.

Develop your ability to:

- Relate **detail** to **broader content, meaning** and **style**.
- **Analyse** and **synthesize** (bring a range of ideas together clearly).
- Understand **implicit** (hinted) **meanings** and **attitudes.**
- Show understanding of the author's **intentions, technique** and **meaning**. (Brief and appropriate comparisons with other works by the same author will also gain marks.)
- Give **personal response** and **interpretation**, backed up by **examples** and short **quotations**.
- **Evaluate** the author's achievement (how far does s/he succeed – give reasons).

*M*ake sure you:

- Use **paragraphs** and **sentences** correctly.
- Write in an appropriate **register** – formal but not stilted.
- Use short, appropriate quotations as **evidence** of your understanding.
- Use **literary terms** correctly to explain how an author achieves effects.

THE EXAM ESSAY

If you are sitting the AQA syllabus you need to be aware of the following details.

Specification A

- does **not** allow you to take a copy of *Enduring Love* into the examination (so you need to know the novel thoroughly);
- gives you 60 minutes to answer the question;
- asks you to answer only **one** question out of the two offered.

It is worth spending 10–15 minutes planning the essay.

Specification B

- is an 'open book' paper so allows you to take *Enduring Love* into the examination (make sure your teacher explains the rules about annotation to you beforehand);
- gives you 90 minutes to answer the question, but some of this will be reading time;
- asks you to answer only **one** question out of the two offered.

It is worth spending 15–20 minutes planning the essay. (You may need to alter this time scale to allow for reading time in the exam, especially if you don't read very fast.)

Planning

An excellent way to plan your essay is in the three stages below, whatever specification or examination board you are doing.

1 **Mind Map** your ideas, without worrying about their order yet.
2 **Order** the relevant ideas (the ones that really relate to the question) by numbering them in the order in which you will write the essay.
3 **Gather** your evidence and short quotations.

You could remember this as the **MOG** technique.

Writing and checking

Then write the essay, allowing 5–10 minutes at the end for checking relevance, spelling, grammar and punctuation, depending on the essay's time limit.

Remember

Stick to the question and always **back up** your points with evidence – examples and short quotations. Note: you can use '…' for unimportant words missed out in a quotation.

Model answer and plan

The next (and final) chapter consists of an answer to an exam question on *Enduring Love*, with the Mind Map and plan used to write it. Don't be put off if you think you couldn't write an essay like this yet. You'll develop your skills if you work at them. Even if you're reading this the night before the exam, you can easily memorize the MOG technique in order to do your personal best.

The model answer and plan are good enough examples to follow, but don't learn them by heart. It's better to **pay close attention to the wording of the question** you choose to answer, and allow Mind Mapping to help you to think creatively and structurally.

Before reading the answer, you might like to do a plan of your own to compare with the example. The numbered points, with comments at the end, show why it's a good answer.

MODEL ANSWER AND ESSAY PLAN

QUESTION

Re-read the section in Chapter 1 of the novel which begins 'We stopped to watch the buzzard ...' (about six pages into the chapter) up to the end of the chapter. What do you think is the significance of this sequence?

Include in your response:

- Joe's response to the events and the way he describes them;
- the treatment of time in the extract;
- the ways in which the image of the balloonist relates to later events in the novel.

(With thanks to AQA GCE English Literature Specification B 20001–2: Specimen Units and Mark Schemes.)

PLAN

- Narrative style: vivid, dramatic, varied.
- Story not continuous, Joe jumps about between past, present and future.
- Introduction to Joe and important themes.
- Balloonist a helpless victim of circumstances – also Logan's literal 'fall' and first link with ideas about the Fall.

ESSAY

The extract from Chapter 1 is significant in a number of ways. Firstly, the shock caused by the accident and Logan's death prepares the reader for the bizarre relationship between Joe and Jed Parry. As well as entertaining the reader with its tense, dramatic description of the accident, it also helps to establish Joe's character, partly because he narrates it in the first person. Furthermore, the image of the balloonist acts as a metaphor for later events.[1]

The spacing before the passage tells us that a new stage of the chapter – and Joe's life – is about to take place.[2] McEwan has already prepared us for this with the urgency of the first few pages of the chapter. In the extract itself, the reference to

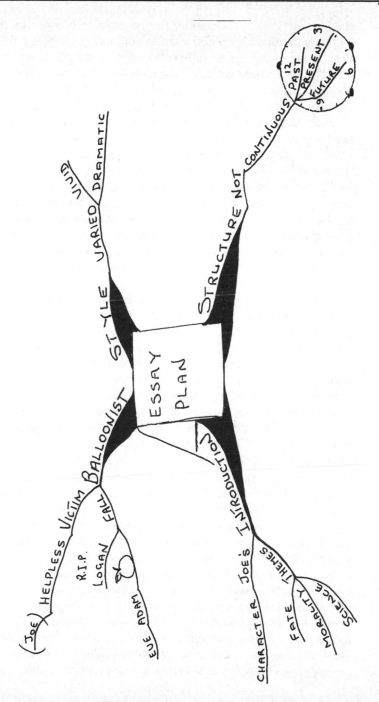

the buzzard acts as a metaphor for the death to come, as if the victim is the bird's intended prey. In addition, Joe's detailed description of the countryside echoes the buzzard's watchfulness. There are other warnings that something bad is about to happen: 'a whole stage of my life closed'.[3]

What is interesting about the extract is that it builds up to a climax – Logan's death – yet the events are not told in a continuous stream. Instead, Joe digresses and jumps around in time, revealing personal details, discussing moral issues and hinting at future problems as well as describing the accident itself. This might seem like an unwelcome distraction but it actually makes the story more convincing and keeps the reader hooked. It is rather like someone telling an exciting story then getting sidetracked. We try to hurry them on, just as we rush through the pages to discover the outcome. Also, because we learn more about Joe and Clarissa they become more 'real' to us, so we care about what happens.[4]

Although the story is told in the past tense, its time-scale can be divided into three. The past before the picnic is described nostalgically. It celebrates the couple's previous 'free and intimate existence'. Secondly, the scene in the fields is written in the past tense but the urgent mood gives it immediacy: 'the wind gusted, and pushed and lifted the balloon ... he was being half dragged, half carried across the field.' McEwan gives strength to the descriptions with the use of other powerful verbs such as 'bumping', 'dig', 'lunging' and 'lurched'. Lastly, the pain of the future is hinted at. 'Later still I discovered ... if I had been ...' The novel is told from hindsight and Joe deeply regrets the tragedy: 'Those one or two ungrounded seconds occupy as much space in the memory as might a long journey up an uncharted river.' Not only do these words suggest the fear and speed of events, they also reveal the terrible repercussions. A few seconds are all it takes to seal John Logan's fate, yet their effects haunt those involved for much longer. The pun on 'ungrounded' also suggests the rescuers' fatal confusion as well as the effects of the wind on them.[5]

The narrative leaps in the passage also give the reader information about other aspects of the story. We are only into the second paragraph when we learn more about the couple's life, including their occasional problems. Later in the extract, Joe expresses complex ideas about human nature's battle between co-operation and selfishness. The accident does not lose its drama in the process, and in fact its seriousness is emphasized because we learn about the agonizing moral choices that often face humans in a crisis. Moral ambiguity is an important theme in the novel, as emphasized in the first chapter. Just as Joe's part in letting go of the rope is unclear, so is his later behaviour questionable, such as when he searches Clarissa's desk or buys the gun.

Joe's guilt that he may have been partly or wholly responsible for Logan's death begins here. The reader is introduced to an intelligent, well-meaning man who wants to do the right thing but is only human. 'It was my duty to hang on ... our misery in the aftermath was proof that we knew we had failed ourselves.' Joe blames the lack of leadership. Everyone acts independently and the result is fatal. As well as the digressions into morality and human nature, the narrative style suggests the speed of Joe's thoughts, rather like an adrenaline rush. Joe is an intelligent man who thinks quickly at the best of times. His scientific background is hinted at in such lines as 'barely a neuronal pulse later' and 'instant calculations of logarithmic complexity were fused'. Yet his quickness makes him act in a manic way at moments of intensity, as with his strange behaviour in Chapters 2 and 9, and elsewhere.[6] The extra details are also an important sign of the thinking that Joe has put into trying to understand the events from hindsight: We get the sense of his analytical mind going into overdrive; he is desperate to make sense of things.

As for the central event, Joe breaks out of his scientific detachment when he personifies the wind. Its actions are made to sound deliberate and evil, not just a random trick of nature: 'the wind renewed its rage ... then it struck ... a mighty fist socked the balloon ... the second more vicious than the first.'[7] The description of Harry Gadd is significant also. The boy's terrified state is called 'learned helplessness', the fear taking away his ability to respond: 'our words were like stones thrown down at his body'. This foreshadows Jed Parry's behaviour later in the novel, because he too blocks out all inconvenient facts about his love for Joe – the truth is too destructive for him to bear.[8]

Harry is frightened of falling and John Logan is actually killed by a fall. This is one of the first allusions to the Fall, the

Adam and Eve theme that recurs in the novel.[9] The balloon accident and Logan's subsequent death push Jed into an odd state, triggering the mental illness that devastates the lives of those affected. Joe and Clarissa's innocent love is destroyed and they are thrown out of the Eden of their relationship into hurt and loneliness.[10]

WHAT EARNED THE MARKS?

1 Good beginning – addresses question and introduces important ideas.
2 Awareness of structural devices.
3 Understands symbolism and uses brief quotations appropriately.
4 Overview of narrative structure and its purpose.
5 Close and detailed analysis of text.
6 Explains how narrative structure can emphasize characterization, and how imagery adds to understanding of character.
7 Appropriate use of literary terms to explain effects of diction.
8 Discusses quotation then places it into context with other parts of novel.
9 Explains significance of balloonist and surrounding events, links it to a central theme.
10 Strong, decisive conclusion.

GLOSSARY OF LITERARY TERMS

allusion   the use of literary, cultural and historical references.

authorial voice   *see* **narrator**.

characterization   the way in which characters are presented.

context   the background of social, historical and literary influences on a work.

epistolary novel   type of novel in which the plot is written in a series of letters.

genre   'rules' of different types of literary work conforming to certain expectations, such as non-fiction, newspaper writing, science fiction, thrillers, etc.

Ideology   a set of ideas that reflects the beliefs of a nation, political system, etc.

image   a word picture bringing an idea to life by appealing to the senses.

irony   a style of writing in which one thing is said and another thing is meant, used for a variety of effects, such as criticism or ridicule.

metaphor   a literary device used for emphasis that describes a thing as if it is something else. A metaphor is like a *simile* but more direct. When original, metaphors give us a fresh look at things by comparing them. e.g. *A shell was forming to protect myself from my conscience.*

narrator   in a novel, a character who tells the story. An *omniscient narrator* has complete knowledge of everything that takes place in the novel, rather like God! An *unreliable narrator* is one whose knowledge and judgements are limited and biased. ✪ Some critics might consider that Joe Rose is an unreliable narrator – what do you think?

oxymoron   a figure of speech that uses an apparent contradiction for emphasis; e.g. Joe describes the sound of London traffic as *tranquillising thunder*, suggesting both its noise and its soothing, familiar qualities.

personification an image speaking of something abstract such as love, death or the wind as if it is a person or a god; e.g. *A mighty fist socked the balloon in two rapid blows.*

plot the story; the events and how they are arranged.

rhetorical question usually used to persuade, not requiring an answer. *Would it have been right … to intrude upon our happiness…?* In this example, Joe is trying to convince himself and the reader that he acted correctly.

simile An *image* that compares things not always associated. It uses 'like' or 'as' as a comparison; e.g. *Our words were like stones.* See **metaphor**.

standard English originating from the East Midlands dialect. It is most often used (and expected) by educated speakers and writers in formal situations such as essay writing. What people sometimes call 'proper' English.

structure the organization of a text such as narrative, plot, repeated themes, images and symbols.

tone the mood created by a writer's choice and organization of words, e.g. angry, persuasive, ironic, detached.

viewpoint the way a narrator approaches the material and the audience.

NDEX

**Page references in bold
denote major character or
theme sections**

AQA syllabus options **100**

characters **10–16**
  Clarissa (Mellon) **12**
  Jed (Parry) **13–14**
  Joe (Rose) **10–12**
  Logan family **15**, 54–7, 83–6
  minor **15–16**
children xvi, **23**, 36–7, 46,
    55, 56, 67, 86–7
criticism **93–7**
  anti-racist 96
  feminist 95–6
  Marxist 94–5
  reviews 96–7

disease and illness **22**, 39,
    48, 53, 59, 64, 78, 89

Enlightenment, The **1–2**
examinations
  hints xiii,
  how to get an 'A' 98–9
  model essay and plan
    100–6

fate **21**, 30, 33, 46, 48, 71

Keats **3–4**, 21–2, 30, 34–5,
    70–1

Language **26–7**, 31, 35, 37,
    40, 41, 43, 48, 49, 51,
    53, 55, 59-60, 61–2,
    64–5, 67–8, 71–2, 75,
    78–9, 81, 82–3, 86, 88
letters 50–1, 60–2, 82–3, 89
love **20–21**, 39, 41, 44, 51,
    53, 55, 64, 67, 81, 88

McEwan, Ian **1**
Mind Maps **x–xi**
morality **22–3**, 30, 42, 56,
    74, 78, 81

non-fiction 9, **26–7**, 86–8

religion and spirituality
    19–20, 34, 36, 40, 53, 59,
    61, 66–7, 78, 86, 88, 89
Romantics, The **2–3**

Setting **27–8**
Science **18–19**, 30, 34, 39,
    41, 42, 45, 57, 61, 70,
    74, 80,
study skills **vii–ix**

109